Mama's Boy

You think Eye'm soft because Eye stick close to my mother,
Failing to realize that she loves me like no other,
Don't fault me because your mother is no longer here,
If she were would you even care?

You live according to societies rules,
Neglecting the fact of the woman who gave you the necessary tools.
A mama's boy is not so bad at all,
So grab your balls and continue standing tall.

When mama needs you're always there,
Just like she is for you so she'd have no fear,
You only get one mother so never forget,
Those calling you mama's boy relationship with their mother didn't mean shit.

Be watchful of those that criticize you through and through
Never turn your back on your mother she's the one that gave birth to you,
Life wouldn't exist if it wasn't for my mother,
Yet feeling some sort of way being called mama's boy by another!!

Take it as a badge of honor and one to be respected,
Did you notice the one's calling you mama's boy are the one's most rejected?
They're sitting back wondering if you'll ever leave mama's side,
Not understanding she's the true "ride or die."

Eye know time is winding up and mama will be no more,
When that time comes it will hurt me to my core.
Just knowing the time shared with mama Eye did my best,
Embracing every moment until its time for her eternal rest.

Until then watch and see,
When you look up it will be my mama and me.
Just seeing mama being able to smile,
Makes my heart want to run a mile.

She battled cancer, a tumor and always fought for me,
Fuck societies rule my mother she'll always be.
Mama, Eye know you're tired but you refused to see us lack,
Enjoy living your life because Eye got your back!!

- written by Lamont Bershawn

Eye've stood inside the Eye of Hell and remained fearless!

Lamont Bershawn

Copyright © 2019 by Lamont Bershawn

ISBN 9781970160017 Ebook
ISBN 9781970160000 Paperback

All rights reserved. No part of this publication may be reproduced, distributed, or transmitted in any form or by any means, including photocopying, recording, or other electronic or mechanical methods without the prior written permission of the publisher. For permission requests, solicit the publisher via the address below through mail or email with the subject line "Attention: Publication Permission".

EC Publishing LLC
11100 SW 93rd Court Road, Suite 10-215
Ocala, Florida 34481-5188, USA

www.ecpublishingllc.com
info@ecpublishingllc.com
+1 (352) 234-6201

Printed in the United States of America

Table of Contents

Introduction 7
God Was Always There 13
You're Going to Hell 36
Conversations 51
Be·tray·al 76
Am Eye My Brother's Keeper? 107
He Left Her for Dead 142
Why Eye Didn't Get Married 153
Aye, Aye 224
Acknowledgements 230
Dedication to Lamont 232

Introduction

During my transition from the church and re-"lie"-gion {religion} many people have told me, "You're going to bust hell wide open."

Well, my first question would be, "Why?" Is it because my thinking changed; my views or because Eye have a different concept when it comes to religion?

Eye've decided to denounce the possessive "I" and begin using the "conscious" Eye which only means that Eye'm viewing things more from within my reality opposed to what Eye've been taught. Eye no longer can deny my truth, my experiences, my nature {NTR}, my mind nor what's in my heart.

"Eye Refuse to Bust Hell Wide Open", is the answer to so many people's accusations towards me when it comes to their be-"lie"-f {belief} system. Eye've awakened and will always walk in my spiritual essence of truth, therefore Eye refuse to conform to anyone's way of life than that of my very own.

Eye've received the ridicule from those Eye call and or consider family, but it's perfectly fine if they'd rather live the "lie" by conforming to words in a book that has nothing to do with them. This particular part of my journey allowed me to focus on the things in life that really matters instead of the trivial things that would cause one to stay upset, angry, confused or depressed.

Eye've realized what the church {Institution/ Insane Asylum} was really about when Eye decided to open my real eyes in order to recognize the real lies being told. Eye can also attest to the fact that most pastors have no clue the messages they're giving to their congregation, all they know is how beneficial the name of the "Lord" is.

Eye've also decided to set aside every religious title that no longer can contain me. Eye'm metaphysically evolving into the masterpiece that my parents co-created.

Are you ready and willing to walk this journey with me?

In this life Eye've learned in order to reach "heaven" you must learn to endure so many obstacles as you go through "hell."

Throughout the book I'll be using "I" in the possessive form which means that I've experienced a particular situation. "Eye" in the conscious form which means that Eye understand exactly what Eye'm seeing or dealing with and "Aye" which means point, period or Aye get it.

During my awakening when I cut ties with the church so much has changed for the better concerning my personal endeavors. My prayer life is different to the point that I don't feel there's a need to bow my head and reverence an outside source; yet I can hold my head held high and appreciate nature and the person Eye've become.

"Do you ever wonder why your prayers constantly go unanswered?

I know some that are in denial will say, "My prayers are always answered!"

NO, THEY'RE NOT!!

The reason is because there's a HUGE difference between "Prayers" opposed to "Will." The church will teach you according to the Bible, "The prayers of the righteous availeth much."{James 5:16}.

Who are the "Righteous?" Answer: NO ONE!

Well, that's the reason YOUR prayers are still in cyberspace or in some other galaxy still waiting to reach its destination. A prayer is a self-released conversation to another being, which happens to be a desire/ want. In other words, you're leaving YOUR desire/ want up to someone/ something else.

When you "Will" something, you summon your desire by the AUTHORITY within YOU. I know there's some who are mad, angry, or upset with God because (1) It allowed your loved one to die

EYE'VE STOOD INSIDE THE EYE OF HELL AND REMAINED FEARLESS!

of cancer or another disease (2) it took your only child from you at a young age (3) it never answered any of your prayers (4) your innocent child is still incarcerated (5) it gave you the wrong spouse, etc.

Whatever the reason is, it wasn't God's fault. God have given you the POWER to DISCERN, THINK, REASON, and make a CHOICE or SOUND DECISION. Stop praying and begin using YOUR "WILL POWER" to summon the desires of YOUR heart. I PROMISE you'll feel better and experience a great change."

People have asked me to pray for them on several occasions. I don't and will never pray again. I understand that never is a long time, but it serves no purpose.

Prayer is a solution to NOTHING!

Prayer ONLY soothes the mind to make an individual feel that some sort of re-"Lie"-f is coming.

Eye have a connection with God.
Eye know God.
Eye understand God.
Eye receive spiritual texts from God.
Eye use the mind that Eye received from God.
Eye don't fear God.
My God is Loyal.

If your relationship with your God isn't similar to anything written above, then you need to re-evaluate who and what you're worshiping.

You are not the creator of you {self}, but you are the author and finisher of your thoughts. You have the power to accept or reject your psychological intake.

You might be going through an emotional period at this moment, but the tears are only cleansing the dirt so that you're able to see clearly and begin focusing.

Never forget that you're an innovator, motivator, conqueror, inventor, creator, mentor and most of all a mother, father, sister or brother.

You create the path to your destiny; don't allow someone or something else to direct you.

Hold on to your seats as we take this ride denouncing religious turmoil getting into our spiritual truth.

In the end you'll be able to say, "Eye know who Eye'm and Eye Refuse to Bust Hell Wide Open!!"

There will be things that you'll read in this book that will actually open your eyes to things you'll recognize about yourself. In any event, it is not my intention to make you think as Eye think, do things as Eye've done or coerce you to believe the way that Eye do. However, it is my intention to get you to think about things instead of taking someone else's way and make it your very own, being final or concrete.

Allow me to say it this way using biblical scripture so some of you can better understand what Eye'm trying to get you to understand.

John 1:1, "In the beginning was the Word, and the Word was with God, and the Word was God."

John 1:14, "And the Word was made flesh, and dwelt among us, (and we beheld his glory, the glory as of the only begotten of the Father,) full of grace and truth."

The Bishop told me that this is how God became Jesus {in the flesh} and was perfect walking/ living in Earth among the people.

My response to this Bishop:

When we look at the beginning of anything, it begins/ starts with a thought, a dream or something that's envisioned. This is the "Word" that have come from within YOUR very being. You're now the CREATOR of THAT "Word/ phrase" that have come from within and is now WITH you.

The "Word/ phrase" cannot become "God" UNTIL the "Word/ phrase" BECOMES a REALITY. When the "Word" that you've thought or envisioned BECOMES a REALITY, then it BECOMES a part of YOUR FLESH because YOU'RE NOW in the PROCESS of Living out YOUR DREAM!!

Here's an example:

You're a child and have a dream, vision or a desire to be on T.V. {this is the WORD that came from within YOU}. You write the

EYE'VE STOOD INSIDE THE EYE OF HELL AND REMAINED FEARLESS!

dream on a piece of paper {Now the words are WITH you because you've made them plain and visual}. You awaken every morning to look at what you wrote down and put every effort to make YOUR dream come true. Twenty- five years later YOU catch a big break and YOUR opportunity to be on T.V. has arrived {Now YOUR PERSONAL words/ phrase became YOUR REALITY, which is what YOU placed in your atmosphere and is a part of YOU.

By SPEAKING it into existence made it YOUR REALITY and became a part of YOUR FLESH because it came from WITHIN YOUR SPIRIT}.

God was NOT "Jesus" in the FLESH, nor was "Jesus" perfect!!

Everyone has their OWN EXPERIENCES with God, NOT to be based off "Jesus" experience or the following of a book.

Look at it like this: Everyone has different goals. There's some that want follow in their parent's footsteps which is perfectly fine "IF" that's where your SPIRIT, PASSION or HEART is.

POINT: YOUR destiny BEGINS from a THOUGHT birthed by YOUR God from WITHIN YOUR spirit. This is EXACTLY why Eye CONSTANTLY say, "God is a PERSONAL Concept that people have made a COLLECTIVE REALITY."

Everyone have a DIFFERENT mindset, level of THINKING, upbringing/ raising and EXPERIENCE in life which will ALWAYS be GUIDED by YOUR PERSONAL God!!

Remember, someone else's ambitions and goals will NEVER work for YOU because they weren't BIRTHED within YOU. YOUR LIFE is NOT to be COMPARED to the Bible because YOU'RE NOT the AUTHOR/ CREATOR of ANY of the BOOKS that were COMPILED in it!!

In this book, we'll become more in touch with our reality opposed to the things we were taught as children and accepted them as being concrete. In the hustle and bustle of daily life people really don't know how to trust themselves. As people, parent's, guardians or leaders it's easier to give the responsibility of our lives over to created entities instead of recognizing our power within or "God's intention" for us to reconnect with our consciousness. People daily hold onto religion and prayer because it's their be-"Lie"-f that a powerful spirit, mediator or divine entity will come to their aide.

"Eye've Stood inside the Eye of Hell and Remained Fearless", is referring to every lie that has been told on me, my period of being incarcerated for protecting my sibling, the countless years of being stabbed in my back, the dismembering of friendships after many years, being disregarded by my own father, dealing with the deadly motives of scorned and mentally disturbed women and my tenure as a Pastor. Many people are "pew dwellers" which means they come to the church and sit in the pew listening to any preacher deliver a message and take it as being concrete. Eye found being a preacher to be a blessing as well as a curse. The blessing portion comes in many forms {teaching, preaching, learning, money, etc.}. The curse is that people will only accept what they've heard a million times over instead of receiving the calculated truth. When the spirit of truth is revealed a preacher must find a way to give it to the congregants using scripture or it won't be received.

Buckle up, sit back and enjoy the ride as Eye take you on my journey through the Eye of Hell. A true and inspirational story of how Eye was able to conquer or overcome every obstacle.

God Was Always There

Being raised in a Christian household, I was taught that there's power in prayer and that "A Family that prays together, stays together."

Living and experiencing life showed me that's really not a fact. You see, I was taught it, but I realize it's a constant phrase used in the church but in essence the word they're using is spelled a little differently- "prey."

THIS IS TOTAL BULLSHIT!!

"A family that prays together stays together!!"

How do I know?

I'm glad you asked. I was a part of a church, religious organization/ affiliation for MANY years. Yes, I've traveled to MANY churches regardless of denomination.

In EVERY ONE of them there were people holding hands in their personal circles, speaking in "unknown tongues" and either smiling or had tears in their eyes for the moment.

I'd sit back with my eyes open because I knew I wouldn't be able to see anything with my eyes closed. I wasn't about to depend on faith because I had enough wisdom to know/ understand that nobody had my back better than ME.

"Wait on the Lord!" Who me? Nah, I knew "his" track record. Too many of my ancestors waited and "he" was a no show. The proof was in the hanging/ lynchings, mistreatment, degradation, etc.

Most of you can attest to the FACT that you've prayed together as a family and most of you can't stand being in the same room together. Don't be fooled into believing that prayer works or makes things happen, IT DON'T!!

As a matter of FACT, some of you don't trust your own relatives, let alone holding their hand in prayer. I know, doing it for "Big Mama's" sake <u>unsure emoticon</u> Pastor Jamal Bryant even said, "THE CHURCH IS THE ONLY ARMY THAT WILL KILL THEIR WOUNDED SOLDIERS!"

What does this mean? The church doesn't really give a flying fuck about you. If you don't believe me, STOP PAYING TITHES/OFFERING and you'll see what the true focus is on.

Let's substitute the word "pray" for "prey." This will get you to understand the truth.

"A family that preys together stays together!"

In this sense, there's no belief needed. This is the real deal because there's an individual, but collective purpose, motive and agenda!!

POINT: It's not the prayer that keeps a family together, it's not the love that keeps a family together, and it's not the "blood" or your belief that keeps you a family. It's the LOYALTY to one another that keeps a family together.

I recall going to the casino with my mother. I'd go with her because I didn't ever want her get robbed or ripped off after hitting a jackpot. I'd also go just to be in the entertaining atmosphere. It seemed like it was a place where people could let down their hair, smile, get great food, meet nice people and have fun. I knew this was one of my mother's outlets and also a stress reliever, not to mention an expensive habit.

Nevertheless, it was a place where we as a family could go and enjoy the company of each other instead of always being confined at home. I mean we used to take family vacations, but all of that seemed to come to a halt when we all got older and began working and developing our own personal lives.

My mother and I went to the casino late one evening. When she went to play her machine I just sat a few machines away and looked around. I remember seeing a few people watching this one particular gentleman who was dressed in a camouflage jacket with rolled up sleeves with his tattoos showing, a pair of combat boots and "camo" pants as if he was read y for battle. I didn't know his name, but he was hitting jackpot after jackpot. I mean, this guy would be so kind that he'd be giving away a portion of his winnings and making sure anyone around him was having a great time.

You knew he had to be a regular customer because he was always playing the same machine, "Treasures of Troy." It was at low a penny machine, but at maximum a forty dollar ($40.00) bet per spin. I see why he always drew so many people's attention because he'd consistently bet the max on the machine. He did it so often they named him, "The Terminator."

Well, after seeing him play and win I began going to the casino just to watch him, while my mother enjoyed playing her favorite machine, "Sun and Moon." As I was standing there he hit another jackpot. When he turned around, he looked at me and said, "You never once bothered me while I was playing. I only have one rule and that's never asking me for anything. "He handed me a fifty dollar bill and said, "have fun." Well, I did what he asked, but didn't win anything of course. I went to go check on my mother and she was doing just fine on her machine. When I went back to watch "The Terminator", he looked at me and smiled. He said come sit next to me. So I did. He extended his hand and said, "Hello, my name is John." I said, Hello Sir. He responded, "Don't call me Sir! I actually worked for a living." {smiling}. My name's Lamont and I'm pleased to meet you. Well, my mother finished playing her machine and came over where I was, so I introduced her to John. John asked, "This is your mother?" I said, "Yes." "She doesn't look like she has a child your age", John replied. We all smiled. John asked mom, "How did you make out? Mom responded, "I lost it all." John then handed her a one hundred dollar bill. Mom said, "No, I can't accept that." John said, "You're Lamont's mother and I see how much he loves and honors you. My mother is gone and it's an honor to bless my friend's mother."

This became more of an eye opener to me and how present God was with all of us at every moment, even without praying. So much has happened in American culture to the point that we begin hating, bashing, ridiculing and degrading people because of skin color.

We've been so blinded by religion that we've lost our true spirituality and essence of the true and living God within our spirit. No one's born with hate, envy or malice in their hearts for another. We're born with love, it's the only thing that's innate; everything else is learned behavior.

I didn't tell you how many people looked at John's appearance thinking he was nothing more than a homeless man or bum playing a slot machine for a penny. John became a good friend, not because of his generosity but because of the wisdom he'd share with me. It took approximately three months of conversing for John to be able to trust me. John said, "I don't judge people I trust them according to what I see them do and how they act or react to certain things."

One evening, I played the machine next to John but it just wasn't hitting. John leaned over {after hitting thirty two jackpots that evening} and said, "Stop playing for a moment. I don't usually do this but what I'm about to say is very serious. He gave me his cell phone number and his home address. You're no longer my friend you're now my younger brother." I was speechless and amazed at the same time. In other words, John accepted me as his family and treated me like such.

John found out that I wrote a book and he ordered five copies upon trying to get the casino to have a book signing for me. When he read the book, he said that we have a lot in common. Most importantly, he wasn't concerned about religion, but the love and respect of humanity.

It was nothing for John and me to have a three to four hour conversation as we shared wisdom with each other. I found out that he loved to help his friends and family, he had a sense of humor out of this world and he didn't accept any nonsense or foolishness. John said, "I sense that you're carrying a weight that's hard to let go." I responded, "I'm okay." He responded, "You Aquarians live according to your zodiac signs. Instead of allowing the water to flow, you'd rather place it in a pitcher and carry it." I laughed.

"When you think you're going through bad shit, just try fertilizing crops without sh{it}! *" - Alexander Hardy*

John loved to read numerous books, watching "flat black" {just staring at the television while it's off}, smoking cigarettes and drinking diet Pepsi. John called me one morning approximately 4

EYE'VE STOOD INSIDE THE EYE OF HELL AND REMAINED FEARLESS!

a.m. and to his surprise I was still up. He asked, "What are you still doing awake?" I responded, "You know Angels don't ever really sleep because they're always on assignment." {Laughing} John said, "That was one of the greatest responses I've heard." I asked him, "Is everything alright?" John replied, "My heart is heavy and I don't understand why?" I said, "Well, let's talk about it to see if we can lighten the load a bit." John said, "You must have caught hell being a preacher, making yourself available all times of the night for people; listening to their stories." I responded, "Yes, but since Eye left the church Eye've gained religious freedom but still love ministry. In other words, Eye'd make myself available for those that need it, without the title. As a Pastor it was important for me to tell people answers according to the bible, but as a friend I'm obligated to tell them the truth."

John said, "Can I ask you a question?" "Of course", John. Well, I always believed that the wages of sin is death. Can you explain it further in detail?

"The wages of sin is death, but the gift of God is eternal life through Jesus Christ." {Romans 6:23}

Ask yourselves:

Would this biblical god actually grant me eternal life, even though he sacrificed his ONLY son?

Answer: HELL NO!!

This passage could very well mean the "proposed" life after your physical death.

Some might be asking, "What is sin?"

You may have seen this: {S} Self {I} Inflicted {N} Nonsense

This is true, but allow me to go deeper.

Sin is defined by "missing the mark." {Hamartia and Hamartano}.

What does "the wages of Sin is death" mean?

Example{s}:

1. Living according to someone else's dreams and misplacing/disregarding your very own.
2. Working so hard to build someone/ something else up that will never be beneficial to you.

NOTE: It's impossible for "Jesus" to have been like YOU because "he" wasn't created like YOU!!

"Jesus" is nothing more than a "wet dream" which means a fantasy occurring in the midst of your sleep.

Eye say, "Awaken!" It's useless to spend a majority of life debating, arguing and dividing over religion and politics.

S/N: ONLY THE THINGS YOU DO FOR SELF {THE CHRIST} WILL LAST!!

POINT: Create something worthwhile now that you can benefit from that will also intrigue others when you're gone. Death only occurs to those that refuse to leave special memories behind in the hearts and minds of others when they physically perish.

"I have to say that I agree with you. Lamont you're a good man and that's why I believe we're connected. You're one that I consider a human being. Human beings respect humanity", John replied.

People have asked me, "Why did you leave the church?" I left the church not the ministry. In the church I lived according to the curriculum which became contradictory to my spirit. People thought that I was hurt by the church or left because I didn't receive a certain title, status or position. The truth is I was tired of seeing "holier than thou" people carrying the titles constantly lie to the people for monetary gain.

I can recall my last few years being in the pulpit either pastoring or preaching a sermon. My spirit and my flesh were constantly in a battle. My spirit no longer wanted to continue to be a part of the "circus" because I was the narrator/ orator and people listened to the bullshit I'd spew from the bible {bye-bull}.

I knew people would listen because 40% were seeking answers outside of themselves because of a bad decision they made; 50% continued following because they didn't want to disappoint their parents, even though they felt it was some shit in the game; 10% really had no comprehension skills whatsoever.

I refuse to lie and say that it wasn't pleasing to my flesh at times or beneficial. I enjoyed being treated like I was part of the "Royal

EYE'VE STOOD INSIDE THE EYE OF HELL AND REMAINED FEARLESS!

Priesthood or family." Yes, I was great at selling the false product known as "Jesus."

I remember receiving a call from a female Pastor that asked for my help to assist her in finding scripture for a theme for her occasion. She just couldn't seem to find what she needed to make sense. I helped her and she was so excited that she couldn't wait until her service the next day. I remember hanging up the phone and preparing my own sermon. The topic of the sermon was, "Eye Refuse to be Bound!"

The next morning when I awakened I knew this would be my final curtain call. Evidently, not because I would physically perish but being defined by religion was going to be dead to me. Don't get me wrong or misinterpret why I still occasionally get involved into heated debates. It's NOT because I'm trying to prove my point, but it's to help others see what really have them walking by "faith" or being blinded by.

When I entered the pulpit that morning I began to have a conversation with "THE LIVING GOD."

GOD:
EYE'VE BEEN PREPARING YOU FOR SUCH A TIME AS THIS. EYE DIDN'T BRING YOU THIS FAR TO LEAVE YOU. THIS MESSAGE WILL CATAPULT YOU INTO A HIGHER DIMENSION THAT WILL RING OUTSIDE THE WALLS OF THIS INSTITUTION.
Me: Why did EYE remain so long?
GOD:
EYE KEPT YOU IN IT SO THAT YOU COULD FULLY UNDERSTAND AND MADE AWARE OF WHOM THE REAL GOD WAS. IT WOULD'VE BEEN HARD FOR YOU TO SEE DUE TO THE STRONGHOLDS THAT WERE OVER YOU. IT'S IMPERATIVE FOR ME TO FINALLY BRING YOU OUT OF THIS SHIT SO THAT PEOPLE CAN GET A GLIMPSE OF THE REAL YOU.
YOU SEE THE DIFFERENCE IS THAT YOU REALLY LOVE TO HELP PEOPLE, NOT FEED THEM THE LIES FOR

YOUR PERSONAL GAIN, NOT PISS ON THEM AND TELL THEM IT'S RAINING.
Me: Let's not prolong this. Eye'm ready!!
{SERMON DELIVERED}!!
{walking out of the church receiving hugs, handshakes and kisses on the cheek}.
Eye get outside of the doors feeling relieved or as if a ton of bricks lifted off of me.
Three familiar beings are standing outside awaiting my arrival with tears in their eyes.
Me: Why were you two outside waiting for me instead of being a part of the service?
GOD:
THAT'S A PLACE FOR THOSE THAT DON'T KNOW WHO THEY ARE OR THE POWER THEY REALLY POSSESS!!
Little did Eye know when Eye walked out of the church for the "Last Hurrah" my spirit, my conscience and MY GOD {GUIDE} would be waiting for me.

POINT: DON'T EVER GET TO A POINT IN LIFE THAT YOU LOSE YOURSELF, YOUR IDENTITY OR YOUR DIGNITY IN ANYTHING THAT'S REALLY NOT BENEFICIAL FOR YOU OR ANYONE ELSE!!

John said, "See, you're proving what was already revealed to me in my spirit. You have so much honor and love for the people that you're being misunderstood. You're a human being. I'm going to say this and then I'm going to clear the line. Human beings aren't judgmental they see people and things clear, it's the religious people that want to make something real that is only a fantasy. Give my regards to your loved ones and your mom, talk with you later brother and thanks!"

Needless to say when I hung up the phone with John I had an "Aye" moment. I finally got it. Here I was conversing and helping him, but little did he know that he also helped me. My "Aye" moment as in I get it now, I understand it better and I can see things in a clearer perspective.

> *"I had a conversation with God {NOT Jesus}.*
> *I asked God, "How did people really come into existence?" I'm not buying this Immaculate Conception, or Adam and Eve theory.*
> *God responded, "I {Spirit} sacrificed myself by IMPLODING!"*
> *When you look around and see people of various walks, you see ME;*
> *Each person REPRESENTS a part of ME {True Spirit of God}!"*

Aye! Eye'm going to make this short and sweet. This might be confirmation to a few people.

You're sitting back wondering why (1) things haven't blossomed yet (2) the seeds you've sown/ planted haven't produced anything (3) everything you put out there seems to backfire, etc.

Well, allow me to put your heart at ease. It's really not anything you've done and it's not that your blessings are being blocked.

The reason why you're not in the progressive stage as of yet deals with who you're connected to. You're being protected because if you were to receive your blessing at THIS moment, you have people that are connected to you that will cost you all of your hard work.

In other words, you're still connected to a few impostors and stagnant folk that are waiting for the opportune time to rob you.

Why? It's because they don't want anything out of life or they want benefit off of all of your blood, sweat, tears and hard work.

POINT: Not everyone will be happy or appreciate your success. It's perfectly fine to cut off, dismember and disconnect from people that aren't beneficial for where you're headed. This includes {but are not limited to} relatives, associates, colleagues, coworkers, FB friends, etc.

A few days had gone by and John called me at 5:00 a.m. I answered the phone and John said, "I hope I didn't wake you up." I responded, "Not at all John are you okay?" "Yes, I'm okay. I had a few more questions concerning forgiveness. You were the only person that I feel could answer them because I feel you're connected to God just by your character, patience and mannerism alone."

"Is there a limit to the times God is willing to forgive a person?" "Absolutely not", John. I know you're a person that follows biblical scripture so allow me to give you my exegetical response first, and then give you my spiritual explanation.

If you look in the book of Matthew, the eighteenth chapter beginning with the twenty-first verse. It reads as follows, "Then Peter came up and said to him, "Lord, how often will my brother sin against me, and I forgive him? As many as seven times?" Jesus said to him, "I do not say to you seven times, but seventy-seven times.

In John chapter eight {what a coincidence}, as John laughed. We're reminded that Jesus stood up for the adulteress as he asked, "Let he that is among you that is without sin cast the first stone?" Yet no one casted a stone, not even Jesus. Jesus stood up and said to her, "Woman, where are they? Has no one condemned you?" She said, "No one, Lord." And Jesus said, "Neither do I condemn you; go, and from now on sin no more." What does this mean? It simply means that there's no limit to forgiving a person.

John, did it ever occur to you as to why Jesus forgave? John replied, "Because he was perfect and knew about the sins of man. Am I correct? You know I find it difficult to always follow scripture. I'm not going to say that you're incorrect, but allow me to show you something using biblical scripture that may give you spiritual revelation.

I want you to understand that it's not my intention to convince, change, control or conquer your way of thought.

This is your personal journey!! In the course of living it, you MUST commune, consult and challenge the innermost part of your conscious. This means that you MUST question the things that you're feeling opposed to just accepting them. You have the power to change your present condition, your atmosphere, the people you deal with/ the company you keep, your mindset and your future.

The reasons you find it hard to live up to Biblical standards are as follows:

(1) You're conforming to something that has nothing to do with you, but because you've been raised on it you consider it as either being absolute, concrete or the "Words of God"
(2) It's IMPOSSIBLE to live out someone else's dream, nightmare, interpretation or belief that wasn't originated from within your spirit
(3) These are the words given to the "Writers" about the "God's" they created for them
(4) Your God isn't speaking the same language to your spirit for the simple fact; your God connects to you spiritually NOT religiously. In other words, what God says to you is PERSONAL, INTUITIVE and INDIVIDUALISTICALLY UNIQUE!! If God wanted everyone to be the same or on one accord, we wouldn't have our individual brains.

It's never my intention to speak negative about the Bible or scripture from it. I too was once a follower and preacher of it. Keep in mind everyone has their own interpretation of scripture, but here's something that may help.

"And, behold, one came and said unto him, Good Master, what good thing shall I do, that I may have eternal life? And he said unto him, Why callest thou me good? There is NONE good but ONE, that is, God..." {Mt. 19:16-17}.

In other words "Jesus" was saying two things here. He wasn't so much concerned with the eternal life aspect of the question. In "Jesus" response he says something that strikes his own attention, "Why call me good?" There's NONE good but one, and that's God.

When interpreted, the first thing "Jesus" refers to himself as NOT being PERFECT, or there are a few things that if you REALLY understood/ knew about me you wouldn't be saying this.

In current term, "You don't know me like you think you do!"

The second thing "Jesus" was saying is that he's NOT God in the flesh.

Understand this: Even "Jesus" took time away from his disciples and everyday people for the purpose of:

(1) RELAXATION (2) REJUVENATION (3) RESTORATION (4) TO REPLENISH (5) RELEASE {SEXUALLY IF NEEDED} (6) REVIVE (7) REFRESH, etc.

NOTICE the prefix "Re?" It means to do it again.

It's imperative to constantly re-evaluate of your life, your friends, your "Family", etc. as everyone/ everything have the tendency to change or REVEAL their true identity to you. As you continue to evolve, it's not always necessary to revolve because that's where you'll find those individuals that want to reminisce or pull you back into a time that you're no longer in.

Keep seeking, researching and studying. The answers you seek have already been given to you within your spirit!!

John was speechless for a moment as he stuttered saying, "Yu, yu, y... You know that is why I knew I could depend on you to answer my question. John, I want you to know that there are levels to forgiveness. If your life, well being or freedom isn't in jeopardy then by all means forgive the person and continue on with a cautious friendship. However if it will compromise your life or freedom; forgive them and cut them off completely.

> *"Forgiveness is a part of the keys to opening the door to a successful life: As Eye've gotten older Eye "real-eyes" that they're levels to forgiving/ forgiveness. It's hard for some people to say, "I'm sorry or I apologize" but they'll reveal their forgiveness through their actions.*
>
> *We must take note that everyone carries a different set of rules according to their raising/ upbringing. Sometimes it's easier to accept what we can get from a person instead of expecting them to apologize "our" way.*

EYE'VE STOOD INSIDE THE EYE OF HELL AND REMAINED FEARLESS!

> ***When we sit back and analyze the situation, we've disregarded, cut off or disconnected from someone that looked up to us. They were learning how to become a better individual just trying to mimic YOU!!" – Lamont Bershawn***

John said, "I couldn't agree with you more." I know I'm talking your ear off and I really appreciate your patience with me. "How do you personally handle betrayal?"

I mean we just spoke about forgiveness, but is it hard to forgive when you've been betrayed?

Now this is a load of bricks…lol. When a person betrays you, it means they disregarded your trust or led you to believe they were capable of being trusted in order to confide in them. I'd say betrayal is literally worse than being stabbed in the heart.

Let me answer this with the perfect quote:

"BETRAYAL is the worst fucking sin; especially by those you once considered kin!" – Alexander Hardy

You never cease to amaze me with the answers you've given me. There were things that I honestly will say that I've carried for decades, but listening to you this morning allowed me to lay my burdens down. I now understand what "God was always there" means. It simply means that God being the center or spiritual essence of where everything derives or originates I have the power within to make things happen for me.

This brings up another question. "Is there a need to pray?" I know a few scriptural references dealing with prayer, one of which Jesus was teaching the Disciples to pray saying, "Our Father…" I often wondered if Jesus taught the Disciples a specific prayer; "Wouldn't that prayer be useful in these times?" I've been to several churches and have even taught to pray in my home, but the prayers are much longer, specific about something or someone and drawn out to the point I'm not sure if people are praying to God or begging for relief.

People are taught or told to pray regarding their religious beliefs. There's never any need to pray and ask for anything. Prayer makes "The Living God" look like a confused, discriminatory bully showing favoritism.

If prayer really worked people would be healed of cancer or any other deadly diseases, innocent people would be freed from prisons, babies wouldn't be born with deformities, etc.

> *"God is not in the prayer answering business, that's why we have power within our Will or Thought,!!" - Lamont Bershawn*

Whether you know it or not there are many forms of "Gods." Many people think the bible is based on one God, about one God and only one God is referenced; but the truth of the matter is that the bible references many Gods.

Here's a list of a few referenced in the bible:

(1) Astroloth - Judges 2:13, Samuel 7:3-4
(2) Baal - 2 Samuel 2:8; 1 Kings 17:1, 18:17-19; 2 Kings 1:2-5; Jeremiah 9:13-16; Hoseah 2:2-13, 14-22
(3) Baal-zebul - 2 Kings 1:2-5
(4) Bel - Isaiah 46:1-4 (also in apocryphal chapters removed from Daniel)
(5) Beelzebub - Mark 3:22
(6) Chemosh - Numbers 21:29, Judges 11:24
(7) "Day Star" and Dawn - Isaiah 14:12-15
(8) Hadad-rimmon - Zechariah 12:11
(9) Ishtar - Jeremiah 44:15-28
(10) Marduk - Jeremiah 50:2-3
(11) Milkom - 2 Samuel 12:30
(12) Nabu - Isaiah 46:1-4
(13) Sakkuth and Kaiwan - Amos 5:26
(14) Tammuz - Isaiah 17:9-11; Ezekiel 8:14-18; Daniel 11:36-39

EYE'VE STOOD INSIDE THE EYE OF HELL AND REMAINED FEARLESS!

We're spiritual beings encased in flesh therefore our spirit is connected to a spiritual or Living God. Religious books encase religious Gods or deities, which only mean the power isn't factual but it only seems that way based only from the power to believe.

What's the difference between Spiritual Gods vs. Religious gods?

A Spiritual God exists internally and is eternal. It can also exist externally but provides an internal life force or supplement for your existence.

A Spiritual God is:

Omniscience which is defined having complete or unlimited knowledge, awareness, or understanding. In other words, all knowing.

Omnipresent is defined as Ubiquitous. Present in all places at all times.

Omnipotent is having unlimited or universal power, authority, or force; all-powerful.

A Spiritual God speaks to your internal essence; therefore needs no written literature or form of external instruction.

A Spiritual God needs no worship, but is glorified:

(1) In spirit and in truth
(2) With deeds from the heart
(3) Out of pure love
(4) Humanitarian work/ freely helping others
(5) Intimately
(6) Without judgment

A Religious god have a false connection of reality through a {be-"LIE"-f} system.

Religious Gods have:

Rules, regulations, doctrine, dogmas, disciplines, guidelines and principles to keep people living in fear.

Mass manipulation using a man made, created myth/ individual to swindle/ enslave the people.

Powerful only by way of manipulation; but have no ability to harm one in reality or in an afterlife.

Psychological Suicide - destroying the intellectual capability of one to think.

Mental Degradation - degrading the intelligence of self and others at all cost.

Religious gods have no connection to YOU and only seem real because of the information received as a child. As a child the illustrations you saw in books as well as the stories you picturesquely formed in your CREATIVE mind {Angels, Demons, Deities, etc.}

Religious gods:

(1) Must be worshiped
(2) Apotropaic rituals
(3) Manipulate
(4) Hidden motives
(5) VERY judgmental
(6) Create scare tactics

POINT/ BOTTOM LINE:

You're a SPIRITUAL BEING!! Allow the Infinite/ Spiritual presence to guide YOU along the path of life. STOP allowing someone else's lifestyle or perceived blessing pull you off course. There's a time and season for ALL things. YOUR time is NOW, so make it happen!!

"No one in the clergy field has ever taken the time to personally answer the questions I've asked in a much precise way than you", John said.

Lamont, there's two types of people living in this world. "There are people and then there are human beings. People are haphazardly walking this earth doing what they want, never taking the time to be a servant of others. Human beings are those that don't mind taking the time to help someone or exemplifying love whenever it's possible." You my brother are indeed a human being. You've taught me so much through this conversation that I actually felt the weights that I've been carrying dropping and the burdens being laid to rest.

EYE'VE STOOD INSIDE THE EYE OF HELL AND REMAINED FEARLESS!

*"**<u>Knowledge is knowing something; Genius is knowing how to apply it, but true wisdom is knowing if and when you should actually make it work!</u>**"* – Alexander Hardy

John and I talked so long that I lost track of time that I had a question of my own for him, not to mention that I didn't want John to think that I was an Atheist. People are so quick to label or categorize a person because they don't or refuse to believe in your religious deity. Eye wanted John to know that Eye knew the Living God" and no longer would confess a book deity, but because Eye had taught and preached in church so long Eye knew where he was in his belief.

Eye asked John, "Who was the first God he came to know?" John paused for a moment and replied, "I'm Jewish, so I don't consider Jesus to be the Messiah, just a Prophet. I understand your question but I know you only asked me to get me to think. I'm going to be safe and say I'm not sure."

What if I were to tell you that your mother was the first God/ Goddess that you came in contact with or came to know? "Hmmmn", said John. "Can you explain that one?"

In my life I know this to be factual/ actual:

There are **THREE MAJOR** Gods that you will come in contact with and MUST adhere to.

The FIRST God/ Goddess is: Your mother; who could have aborted you, but made the decision to give you life.

The SECOND God is: Nature {spiritually/ physically in tuned to you}

The THIRD God is: Your consciousness, your intuition or that INNER VOICE that will guide you throughout life.

Allow me to take this a bit deeper where we both will be able to see this a little more clearer, because most people subscribe to religion based on how they were raised.

"Do we really need religion to guide us?" ABSOLUTELY NOT!!

The characters mentioned in your religious books of choice have no power over what happens to you, with you, by you, because of you and therefore have no say/ power over the consequences given you.

It's time for us to destroy the generational curse that plagued us. We have been following the guidelines of religion {re-LIE-gion} to the point that most of us are NO EARTHLY GOOD.

I guess most would ask, "Why would you say that?" Don't you think religion helps to keep people in line or in a controlled environment?" Control is key!!

What is religion?

Religion {Re-LIE-Jun} is a bullshit belief system that was created to:

(1) Make one deny their own spirituality
(2) Confuse people to the point that they rely on something outside of themselves
(3) Degrade the intellect of SELF
(4) Prepare oneself for an Insane Asylum by becoming institutionalized
(5) Teach people how to become imprisoned in their own minds!"

Religion makes people lazy and crazy. If you don't agree with me, it's perfectly fine.

Just check this out.

ASK YOURSELVES:

1. Who was the very first God/ Goddess you were introduced to? Answer: Your Mother.
   Those of you that refuse to see your mother as a Goddess:
      (a) Did she have the power to abort you? Absolutely!
      (b) Did she have the power to bring you into existence? Absolutely!
      (c) Did she provide for your internal system/ carrying you for nine months? Absolutely!

EYE'VE STOOD INSIDE THE EYE OF HELL AND REMAINED FEARLESS!

When you were born, you knew your mother based on her scent, touch and unconditional love.

{MOST PEOPLE HAVE GIVEN THEIR CHILDREN OVER/ RELINQUISHED THEIR PARENTAL GUIDANCE TO RELIGION AND THAT PERCEIVED DEITY VIA. AN APOTROPAIC RITUAL WITHIN A RELIGIOUS ORGANIZATION. NOW, THEY'RE WONDERING WHAT HAPPENED?

2. How many people do you know have seen Jesus? NOBODY!!!.... BUT:
    (a) Will give up their all and all for him
    (b) Gives him undeserved credit for your personal accomplishments
    (c) Will give up their lives for him {some say...lol}
    (d) Will sacrifice their own child{ren}
    (e) Sad to say but are actually in a mental institution behind religion?

The POWER is within all of us to make this a better place to live.

LOOK AT SELF: YOU have the power to LOVE; YOU have the power to HELP; YOU have the power to stop backbiting; YOU have the power to stop murdering; YOU have the power to CREATE, INNOVATE, INVENT, BUILD and make choices.

The power ISN'T in the prayer, but the power IS within YOUR WILL TO MAKE IT HAPPEN!!

YOUR "Will power" is so much more powerful than prayer. When people begin to understand they have the power within themselves, they'll become more powerful individuals based on their creative minds.

John responded, "That make so much sense to me." I would read the bible and have so many questions because so many things just didn't sit right with my spirit. You have just given me the right to acknowledge there isn't anything wrong with my comprehension and for that I want to say, "Thank you brother."

> *"I cannot persuade myself that a beneficent and omnipotent God would have designedly created parasitic wasps with the express intention of their feeding within the living bodies of Caterpillars."* – Charles Darwin

"What God should we really worship?"

I know many people are looking at the question and are probably saying, "There's only one God, who is considered to be the Alpha and Omega {The Beginning and End}!!"

Answer: The "God" that you feel SPIRITUALLY connected to.

Allow me to explain it like this: Many people have gotten so entangled into reading literature, information, books, scriptures, texts, etc. about a "God" or deity. In the process you've gotten so caught up into "Praising" or "Worshiping" this God to the point that you believe that if you don't, this God will turn "ITS" {Respectfully} back on you.

This sort of repetitive/ recycled behavior is part of EVERY {Be - LIE - F} system. {I know some have stopped reading because you believe that I'm blaspheming the name of God}.

First, to ease your minds let's take a closer look at the word "Blasphemy." Blasphemy is a crime committed if a person insults, offends, or vilifies the deity, Christ, or the Christian religion. It can also go against sacred writings, "Biblical Scripture" which some assume to be "God's Word."

When one gives "Perfected" thought into what blasphemy consists of, it's considered to be contrary to the "Holy Spirit." The "Holy Spirit", according to the Free Dictionary is the third person of the Trinity. When one engages in extensive research/ study, the "Holy Spirit" is considered "Divine Wisdom."

To blaspheme is to DENY the spirit of YOUR own thought, conscious/ conscience, or mindset. To hear, feel, or KNOW inner TRUTH through your senses or meditation; yet DENY all of "IT" because of what's written inside of a book. You're more valuable, more important and more sacred than ANY book; therefore YOUR

CONNECTION to God holds more weight than what you're reading and NOT understanding!!

Now that I've clarified blasphemy, let's get into the man made "Gods" people worship daily, seasonal, or just in the institution{s}. In the month of December, when many people spend lots of money going to the various malls/ shopping center and take their children to see "Santa Claus."

The story goes as follows, "He knows if you've been bad or good, so be good for goodness sake" because if you don't, you won't be blessed with gifts. In many monotheistic religions {Islam, Judaism, Zoroastrianism, Deism, Christianity, certain sects of Hinduism, Sikhism, etc.}, if a "God" isn't worshiped, the belief is that you'll be sent to a place of eternal punishment in the "Afterlife."

Please make note of this that a "God" is NOT limited to religion.

"God is a PERSONAL concept that people have made a COLLECTIVE reality."

What God should be worshiped?

ANSWER: "The LIVING GOD!!"

Who is the "LIVING GOD?"

It's the GOD that don't stoop to the level of frivolous actions; it's the God that's constantly/ consistently being worshiped through the positive actions/ love of humanity; it's the God that's embedded so far deep within the minds/ hearts of the people that's being overlooked by {Re – "LIE" - Gion} and overshadowed by hate.

Just how POWERFUL is God?

Is God so powerful that "IT" can create the Universe, but can't stop the violence on Earth?

Is God so powerful that "IT" can plant trees that can exceed 200 feet, but can't bring a murderer to justice?

Is God so powerful that "IT" can put oceans in place, cause tornadoes, hurricanes, tsunamis, etc. that can cause so much destruction in the land; but can't keep a world at peace?

Who is this powerful God, Deity, Entity or Being?

Is it Allah, The God of the Bible, Buddha, etc.? Absolutely NOT!

Certain powers come by way of MANIPULATION. The One TRUE and LIVING God is that of the Infinite Mind, our COLLECTIVE consciousness, supreme soul and existence.

POINT: It is YOU that have the power to bring peace on Earth; it is YOU that have the power to stop the violence and murder. Stop looking unto the hills because YOU are your source and Help at ANYTIME/ ALL the time!!

"You've said a mouthful. Now I understand why it was imperative for you to leave the church", replied John. The church promoted Jesus in a "right now" sort of way, but you directed people to look deeper within themselves, which actually make more sense.

John and I have had several conversations in the past but none as in depth as this one going into detail concerning religious views because I know how friendships are broken due to political and religious views. I recall one of our conversations when John and I were sitting next to each other at the casino. A gentleman walks up to him, taps him on the shoulder {which he hates} and asks John, "Can you have mercy and spare a few dollars so I can play one of these slot machines? I can see you're doing well on your machine. John looks at me and say, "Pardon me for the words you're about to hear come out of my mouth, Bishop." John looks at the gentleman and asks him, "Are you a Christian?" He says, "Yes, but what does that have to do with anything?" Well, if you're a Christian put your belief to work. Doesn't the bible say, "God shall supply all of your needs according to His riches in glory?" It means that you have the ability to receive the desires of your heart without asking anyone for it.

> ***"If you want mercy look between masturbation and murder, but don't look at me!" – Al Hardy***

At the very least John and I understood each other's spiritual views and religious perspectives. John stated, "In the end we'll all come together and be as one." When our lives no longer serve as the purpose of the reason we were created, then we've become obsolete. Nature understands this concept, but people with our limited perception will never get it.

> *"Nature refuses to let its own suffer, but people find joy in watching their own suffer. In my personal assessment of the spiritual God; Its Divine Wisdom omits one to suffer. The religious God will have it no other way than to have one enslaved and suffer, refusing to live beyond its written word." – Lamont Bershawn.*

You're Going to Hell

WHEN EYE WAS PART OF the church, there wasn't a day that had gone by when Eye didn't hear someone tell another, "You're going to hell." My first thought would be, why would that person condemn them to a place of torture?

What Eye was taught about hell growing up, scared me so much that it was hard to go to sleep at times. All Eye could visualize was this red figure made up of pure fire, carrying a pitchfork wearing horns. Eye was told in order to stay out of the pit of hell or the fiery furnace {where Eye'd be burned and tortured but could never die}, Eye had to trust "God's word" which was supposedly the written Divine instructions through the Bible.

Eye would read it so much that certain scripture became repetitive and a part of my daily life. "No weapon formed against me shall prosper", "The Lord is my shepherd, Eye shall not want" and "The Lord is my light and my salvation, whom shall Eye fear." These were the three basic scriptures Eye'd use for protecting me from harm and the devil.

Dealing with the fear- based theologies, the scare tactics and religious doctrine for many years made me challenge everything Eye was taught. Eye came to understand this created God was based on fear and not love. As a matter of fact, all of the religious Gods seemed to have hell within, would throw serious tantrums when things didn't go their way and bipolar tendencies. The offspring or mediators of the religious Gods were calm, considerate and collective.

EYE'VE STOOD INSIDE THE EYE OF HELL AND REMAINED FEARLESS!

Eye recall having a conversation with a Pastor of a "Mega" church.

CONVERSATION:

Me: Hello Sir! How are you
Pastor: Good afternoon Sir
Me: Very beautiful church.
Pastor: Why thank you. God is good!!
Me: You mean to tell me God actually tossed money bags out of heaven?
Pastor: {laughing} of course not!! I've been in full time ministry for thirty years. All I ever do is pray and thank the good Lord for providing. They have provided a church that seats 20,000 people at a time for three (3) services; a million- dollar home; a private jet; food on the table and two (2) half a million- dollar vehicles.
Me: Excuse me Sir, but you said, "They!"
Pastor: Yes! "THEY" meaning the people.
Me: So, the people are considered "God's?"
Pastor: Absolutely!! They have the power to make choices.
Me: Why do you preach about a "Jesus" if you consider them to be Gods?
Pastor: If the people are silly enough to believe in a person they'll never see, who am I to change their minds? I'm benefiting from their ignorance.
Me: Wouldn't it be easier to explain that God has given them the power within, instead of telling them to wait on the Lord?
Pastor: Hell no!! I'm going to milk the superficial product until their giving cease. Change and truth are two things that are hard for people to accept. If they have already received the lie, keeping giving it!
Me: Wouldn't they accept the truth if you taught it?
Pastor: Nope!! You can't give them what they're not ready for.

> *"Religion taught people to denounce themselves the credit they rightfully deserve. Any leader will cash in on a person's ignorance at any given time. Learn to discern with your God given spirit and you'll always come out on top."* – Lamont Bershawn

Eye've always been skeptical when it came to the teachings of Hell. It's easy to induce a child's mindset with fear and scare tactics, just as it was easy to give them a false imagination of Santa Claus and the flying reindeer with a red shining nose. The problem with the lie is that they go on many years believing this to be actual and factual, which in turn does two things. First, it destroys their mental state once they find out the truth and second, it makes it hard for them to trust you {the parents}.

PLEASE UNDERSTAND:

WHEN YOU DIE, YOU WILL NOT GO TO A PLACE CALLED HEAVEN OR HELL.

FACT:

YOUR FLESH WILL DECAY, BUT YOUR SOUL/ SPIRIT WILL LIVE ON FOREVER. WHEN YOUR SOUL DEPARTS FROM THE FLESH, IT NO LONGER HAS ANY MEMORY OF THE BODY IT WAS LIVING WITHIN.
THE BRAIN CARRIES ALL MEMORY AND IT'S STILL INSIDE OF THE DECEASED CORPSE {UNLESS YOU'VE DONATED IT TO SCIENCE, ETC.}
YOUR SOUL IS LIKE THE AIR YOU BREATHE. IT CANNOT BE BURNED.
EXERCISE:

EYE'VE STOOD INSIDE THE EYE OF HELL AND REMAINED FEARLESS!

LIGHT A MATCH, TORCH OR A LIGHTER AND SEE IF YOU HEAR THE AIR SCREAM OR HOLLER.

IGNORANCE {THE BULLSHIT}:

STOP ALLOWING THE CHURCH LEADERS TO PLACE ILLOGICAL, FOOLISHNESS IN YOUR HEAD ABOUT A DEVIL AND A PLACE WHERE YOU'LL BURN FOREVER AND CAN'T DIE.

"WHEN YOU DESIRE TO RID YOUR MINDS OF THE SLAVE MENTALITY; WHEN YOU STOP LIVING ACCORDING TO FEARFUL BELIEF SYSTEMS; WHEN YOU BEGIN PLACING LOGIC OVER RELIGIOUS TEACHINGS IS THE POINT WHEN THE LIVING GOD WILL BE ABLE TO USE YOU!!" – *Lamont Bershawn*

The fascinating thing about death is the fear the church place on an afterlife. There are many questions that comes into play when the thought of a place with "Pearly Gates" or an "Eternal fire." Get this, you'll feel it {gnashing of teeth} but you can't ever die.

My initial question would be, "How will my soul burn?" The reason Eye'm asking is the nerves and nerve endings are connected to the body or flesh and when it's dead my soul/ spirit will depart and remember my experience in that body no more.

One particular movie that comes to my mind is, "Down to Earth" starring comedian, Chris Rock. He was an aspiring comedian that somehow got in the way of death and died. When he got to "Heaven", he demanded to get back to Earth because "God and the Angels" made a mistake. Looking through the list, the Angel realized they made a mistake, so they decided to send him back to Earth, but the only problem was that he couldn't get back into the same body. No, the body wasn't beat up, destroyed or lost. The reason the Angel gave was because his soul had been out of his body too long. WOW!!

Now, this is where reality sets in. How is it that he couldn't get back into his original body, but "Jesus" could be dead much longer, but could get back into his very own body? Let's not forget Lazarus, who also was able to get back into his body.

The REAL RESURRECTION {SERMON}:

There comes a point in life when you must learn to disregard the negative things that people speak. You must understand that your journey has NOTHING to do with anyone NOT willing to enhance your purpose/ vision or ANYONE that can't take YOU to the next level.

You're going to have the "Naysayers" or the critics that will try to stump your growth, plant the negative seeds or just talk shit because they don't have a fucking thing going for themselves.

In this particular time of your life, if you never hear, understand or accept a word that I speak. Always remember this, "God created YOU for a purpose." God also instilled within YOU a PERSONAL vision, goal or dream with "YOUR NAME" on it." There's going to be people that will come across your path in order to destroy, ridicule or try to discourage you from following your heart.

God will NEVER instill within you such a talent or gift for it to lay dormant!!

The time is now to rise above the shadows, from behind the walls of confinement and from beneath the ground from that "Dirt nap."

Rise up my brother and my sister, so YOUR LIGHT will forever shine!!

The time is now to look in the face of DEFEAT, DORMANT, DICTATE,

EYE'VE STOOD INSIDE THE EYE OF HELL AND REMAINED FEARLESS!

DAMNATION, DEVIATION and DESTRUCTION in order to speak these words, "You should have killed me when you had the opportunity."

Never again will I take low, bow down or get on my knees to pray in the midst of danger or the cunning attack of the enemy.

Eye realize now that bowing my head is a symbol of defeat where no answer shall befall me. I shall keep my head held high knowing that I'm not only a conqueror, but also victorious!!

You'll NEVER be able to see, view or visualize a TRUE/ REAL RESURRECTION until you're able to resurrect YOUR mind or way of thinking.

HOW CAN YOU BECOME RESURRECTED WHEN YOU HAVE NO CLUE THAT YOU'RE EVEN DEAD? - Lamont Bershawn.

"Where Is Hell?"

In my assessment of hell; it is located somewhere between insanity, fantasy and the bullshit one created in their own lives or accept from another. The truth of the matter is that everyone experiences some form of hell due to the negative energy or circumstances involving them.

Do I literally think that hell is a place of torment after one physically leaves Earth? Absolutely not! Why? Well, it's quite simple that the spirit/ soul departs the flesh but the corpse remains. In other words, the organs are still left inside of the body {brain, lungs, heart, etc.} unless of course it's being donated to science. Eye think once the soul departs the flesh, it no longer remembers anything that was once connected to it. All of the family members, friends and loved ones are all forgotten about. The hurtful part is those that are left behind get to remember the good, bad and indifferent concerning the deceased.

According to the bible, hell has different names such as Hades, Tartarus and Sheol. Let's examine these names and take a closer look at their location. We must first take note of the words definition and its origin.

Hades, was the Greek God of the underworld. Sounds familiar or similar of the location the bible uses? The bible references Hades to be the grave. Its origin comes from the word "Head" in English, late 17th century: perhaps a dialect form of the verb head. {Head--------→ Hade}.

Tartarus, was the deep abyss that is used as a dungeon of torment and suffering for the wicked and as the prison for the Titans. Tartarus was both a primordial deity that existed before the Olympians, as well as a name to describe a region of the Underworld. Tartarus was located beneath Hades and was used as the most horrible prison. He was the Greek God that was third in rank after Chaos.

Sheol, refers to the grace or abode of the dead. When the Hebrew scripture were translated into Greek in ancient Alexandria around 200 BC, the word "Hades" (the Greek underworld) was substituted for Sheol, and this is reflected in the bibles New Testament where Hades is both the underworld of the dead and the personification of the evil it represents.

Does anyone else see how most of what's written in the bible was stolen from Greek Mythology? Nowhere in any of the aforementioned places does it mention bodies being burned in an afterlife and impossible to die.

> *"Religion is for people who are scared to go to hell. Spirituality is for people who have already been there."- Bonnie Raitt*

The fascinating thing about Hell that is taught in Christianity is that it's the place where this evil creature called Satan resides. I look at Hell the same I visualize Glory. Remember how the bibles states, "God shall supply all of your needs according to His riches in glory?" {Phil. 4:19} I always wondered where glory was.

EYE'VE STOOD INSIDE THE EYE OF HELL AND REMAINED FEARLESS!

Eye recall making a Face book post asking, "Which statement is true- God loves us or Satan loved us?" Eye received an overwhelming response with over six hundred comments. The answer came out that both statements were true. What most people fail to realize is that the "Devil" and "Satan" are two different beings {look up Angelology}. The original story is that the "Devil" was kicked out of heaven while Satan was commissioned to the Earth to watch over man {Gods creation}. {research The Mighty Grigori}.

> *"Regardless of your chosen faith, at the end of your life's journey, your heart will be measured in two ways. One, the weight of your conscience must far outweigh the weight of a feather. Two, any impurities in your heart must weigh no more than one feather. The purer your heart, the lighter your spirit will be. The lighter your spirit, the closer to light it will float. The closer to light it is permitted to go, the higher it will float. The higher it floats, the closer to God you will be. Heaven has seven layers. The vibrations of your good deeds, which will be reflected by the weight of your conscience and the purity of your heart, will determine the layer in which your soul will reside. Your goal is to make your heart as light as a feather. The heavier the heart, the more chained to this hell it will remain."- Suzy Kassem, Rise Up and Salute the Sun: The Writings of Suzy Kassem*

Have you ever experienced going through a situation in the court or judicial system? If so, that was your "hellified" experience. Why? Because they took a real situation with a Judge and jury but expect you to first "come clean" psychologically with a religious deity that have no regard or any clue as to who you are.

The key is to get you to be psychologically convicted or bound by swearing or affirming by placing your right hand on the bible {religious book}. "Do you swear to tell the whole truth and nothing but the truth? **SO, HELP YOU GOD!**" Personally, Eye've seen many people swear on bibles or any other religious book and blatantly tell lies. The kicker is that the liar won't be punished by the court or religious deity.

Allow me to explain deeper and in detail how the court is designed to take you through hell and burn you at the stake. The District Attorney {D.A.} or better known at the "Devil's Advocate" is to build a case against you using fabrications, lies, portions of probabilities and possibilities without sound facts. The Judge acts as "God" and the jurors are supposed to be council that listen for reason to make a sound judgment call. If convicted or found guilty, but really are innocent; you're experiencing a "hellified" moment that may cause years of distress, psychological despair, physical implications, financial strain and may even cause one to commit suicide.

It really seems that if there was a hell, it's present here on Earth. The problem is that most people are looking for help outside of themselves, when the real power is within the mindset. We have the power to make choices and decisions that govern our ability to progress in life. Hell is a superficial place that most people make their permanent habitat.

PLEASE don't allow the media to intoxicate your minds with "Orange is the new black."

Orange being the new black only signifies/symbolize the acceptance of mass incarceration of black people.

How about Red being the new black signifies the genocide of the Native Americans and blacks?

If black people don't care about their own lives NO ONE else will.

They're the ones that paid the ultimate price with their lives for a country that really don't give a flying fuck about them!

> *"Historically, slavery was the worst thing to ever happen to a people and most slavery was mental, rather than physical. One of the biggest side effects of slavery is the fact that it*

EYE'VE STOOD INSIDE THE EYE OF HELL AND REMAINED FEARLESS!

made us afraid to take responsibility for our own destiny. Many brothers and sisters today still do not want the responsibility that comes with nationalism and true revolution." – **Dr. Umar Johnson**

"Hell is located inside of the church and religious books that keep people enslaved and relying on false gods to take action for real problems." – Lamont Bershawn.

In my opinion Eye'd clearly say that religion is the portal to Hell. Religion speaks about so many different deities or gods with personal issues, humanistic emotions that are ready to condemn people without forgiveness. This is why the majority of religions have mediators to intercede for man. God won't forgive you, but the mediator will because he's the one that supposedly sacrificed his life for everyone.

"Could Hell be located here on Earth?" We could somewhat agree that it is due to the countless number of murders taking place, people protesting and praying but still no sign of a powerful God that could put an end to it all. We witness different countries willing to attack other countries putting innocent women, men and children in the heart of a war over two individuals that just can't seem to agree.

Could the sun be considered to be Hells everlasting fire? We could somewhat agree that the sun is powerful and we need it to continue living. We receive solar power, food energy, happiness, warmth, light and Vitamin D from the sun and without it we'd be non-existent. People have traveled all over the planet, but no one has ever landed on the sun. The amazing fact is that the sun is ninety- two million miles away from the Earth yet it has enough power to cause fires, physical burns and blindness.

Throughout all religious teachings, "Hell" is considered a place of torment. Clearly no one has ever come back from a physical death back into life and can attest to what has happened on the other side. Eye've been in church all of my life and have seen more negativity inside of the church than outside of it. There's a higher rate of divorce by people that attend church opposed to those that just don't go. In my strongest opinion Hell being considered a place of torment would definitely be the religious teachings in the church. Most will disagree with the belief that people gain values, morals and structure by way of biblical teaching. Eye guess that would depend upon the mentality of the individual receiving the "instructions." The bible {buy-bull} main purpose was to control the mass by mental incarceration or slavery, waiting for a mythical deity to show up in order to free them from bondage.

> *When Eye was in tuned to religion Eye saw demonic spirits, all different formations of God's, heard all types of sermons being preached, saw people possessed like never before and all of it taking place INSIDE of the church. All of the apotropaic rituals being followed and still no sign of Jesus. When Eye left the church, Eye was totally setting myself free from the negativity that consistently was brewing inside of the church. Eye realized that Eye had very little or a limited knowledge of self because Eye was conforming to the likes of everyone else and the manipulating force had a stronghold on me. When Eye walked out the church doors for the very last time my spirit was standing next to God. Eye asked them both, "Why aren't you guys inside the church?" God responded, "It's not a dwelling place of mine, that's a place for those that have no clue who EYE really am." -
Lamont Bershawn.*

Many of my friends, family members and colleagues in ministry still believed very much in a literal place called, "Hell." Eye was no longer a subscriber of Hell, nor did Eye believe that Eye'd bust Hell wide open because Eye no longer believed.

EYE'VE STOOD INSIDE THE EYE OF HELL AND REMAINED FEARLESS!

People that called themselves Christians that supposed to be loving and forgiving were the main ones calling me the Anti-Christ because Eye walked away from the church and religious doctrine. This is when Eye knew that it was a blessing to have the knowledge but it was a curse too. Most people don't bother to research information, they're so used to accepting a preacher's word especially if they've heard the same repetitive phrases from church to church.

What if everything in religion was just the reciprocal of what was being taught to you?

Example: "God" and "Satan" roles were TOTALLY opposite of what you were taught?

Could it be the one considered "God" in the bible cause more atrocities and "Satan" really is the one that loved man and wanted to help man?

Something to take to YOUR Pastors:

Often times we hear of the mark of the beast, who is considered the "Anti-Christ." The mark of the beast {according to the bible} carries the number "666."

Let's define what "Anti-Christ" really means:

(1) *An enemy of "Christ." {translation is the enemy of oneself}*
(2) *{"Anti" - opposing/ against} {"Christ" - anointed one}*

In other words, the "Anti-Christ" is an individual going against the anointed one. If you're DENYING your anointing or going against it, YOU'RE considered the "Anti-Christ." You'd better recognize!!

Who is/ are the "anointed" one{s}? Answer: YOU ARE!!

{Eye know it will be some that will reject this because they can't fathom a thought that they even have the power within themselves to THINK or make changes.}

The story goes as follows. "Jesus" became the "Christ" after the "resurrection."

NOTE: the death was NOT a physical death, but it was a spiritual one. The "resurrection" meant that "he" came into knowledge of SELF from a dead level {denying the power within}.

Let's look at the "mark of the beast." (666).

"Here is wisdom. Let him that hath understanding count the number of the beast: for it is the number of a man; and his number is Six hundred threescore and six." - {Revelation 13:18}.

"666 refers to the Wisdom of man!!" {when "he" awakens}.

When "man" no longer feels the need to conform to "Re-LIE-Gion" he will awaken the "beast." He now recognizes/understands and have come to KNOW the power within, therefore he will begin to see the TRUTH where the foundation of lies began.

Eye AM a BEAST and my name is, Lamont Bershawn.

When Eye was Pastoring, Eye found it hard to teach the truth or a different perspective because the curriculum was very precise when it came to preaching the death, burial and resurrection of Jesus. My main goal was trying to keep the congregants from believing in a place of forever torment and look within the confines of their own spirits. Eye'd constantly ask, "Do God need a mediator in order to give you a message? Do God need an instruction manual for you to read and follow? If you were never introduced to any religious information concerning any deity would you know who God is? Of course, your spirit can't ever disconnect from the Creator of it.

Brain Teaser:

What exactly is the meaning, "God has the victory?" When one study the original story as to how "God" wanted humans to be imbeciles, but Satan wanted to give humans knowledge and a better understanding of life's perspectives. Eye guess one would ask, "Why would Satan want to give humans knowledge?"

Truth: Satan was NOT a deceiver! "He" was actually commissioned by "God" to be a "Watcher" of humans. Satan and "ITS" band of Angels knew that humans were illiterate and knew NOTHING. Satan didn't like to waste "ITS" time, so Satan and the other Angels {The Grigori} began to teach the humans how to read, write, make weapons, numerology, astrology, etc.

In other words, Satan disregarded "God's" instructions. "God" only asked Satan to watch over "HIS" creation, NOT to teach them ANYTHING.

Many would think that the "Devil" {NOT Satan} is winning the war because of all of the negative things that are taking place; but the truth of the matter is "God" has already won the battle by planting/ creating the seed of IGNORANCE {according to biblical texts/ scripture}.

Jesus said, "My people are destroyed for lack of knowledge..." {Hosea 4:6}. This brings up another point. How could Jesus be consid-

ered the "Only begotten Son of God", if these particular Angels were also called the "Sons of God?"

POINT: Know the origin of the "God" you serve. They may NOT have as much "Power" as YOU possess. STOP demoting SELF to powerless "Gods!!" – Lamont Bershawn.

Conversations

In this particular chapter Eye expound on the numerous conversations, communication and dialogue with the people concerning religion and God.
 THIS IS GOING TO BLOW YOUR MIND:

As you all may KNOW that Eye'm ALWAYS communicating with MY "God."

Here's the conversation:

ME: Why is it so hard for people to break away from religion?
GOD: They were taught that it's a source of love.
ME: Well, aren't all of the "Gods" a source of love?
GOD: {smiling} YES, in a sense; but more of mind manipulation and control. Those "Gods" seem to throw tantrums when things don't go their way.
ME: What makes you any different?
GOD: Eye want you to understand this and spread this message. The distinct difference between ME and the other gods is that Eye'm LOYAL. LOYALTY is everything to ME.

The other gods had mediators they turned their backs on. It's IMPOSSIBLE for me to turn my back on you and infiltrate everything you're about, without doing it to self.

Love can be bought.

ME: How can love be bought?
GOD: Take an individual that don't understand what love is, or one that have been disowned, disregarded or denounced. They in turn purchase a puppy. Sooner or later they'll feel the love from that puppy. Why? It's because the puppy naturally will become attached to them and will be loyal because love was exemplified.

It's impossible to love without being loyal. Pick up any of the religious books and you'll find where each of those gods were disloyal or had favoritism. Go to any church and the focus is more on the money because there's NO LOYALTY!!

ME: Eye appreciate you for opening my eyes once again.
GOD: It's my honor and pleasure. If your eyes aren't opening more each day or you fail to become wiser, the weight falls on me but will show through you.

EYE CAN SAY, "EYE LOVE YOU" UNCONDITIONALLY BECAUSE OF MY LOYALTY!!

"The Barber"

WTF: I just finished getting into a heated debate, discussion, disagreement with my barber.
Barber: What do you think of the incident in the SC church?
Me: I think it was very wicked for the guy to go into the church and kill nine people. This is why many Pastors either carry a firearm or have personal security.
Barber: Are you serious? How crazy is that?
Me: What do you mean?
Barber: A Pastor should live according to the bible and trust in God with their whole heart. God is a protector!

EYE'VE STOOD INSIDE THE EYE OF HELL AND REMAINED FEARLESS!

Me: Well, explain to me why in the hell that Pastor wasn't protected by God?

Barber: It was just their time to go. We're all going to go, we just don't know how, when or by what.

Owner: {says to barber} "You don't want to engage in that conversation with him."

Barber: Where's your faith?

Me: In me. Eye know me, therefore Eye don't have to depend on any outside force, deity or Savior.

Barber: So you don't believe in God?

Me: Eye don't have to because Eye know the God of me.

Barber: The bible says....

Me: That's how Eye know that you're programmed into a systematic belief system that have psychologically robbed you into being robotic, while awaiting a Savior

Owner: {shaking his head, speaking to barber} "Leave it alone. He's about to go in deeper on you."

Barber: Let's go there then

Me: Are you carrying a concealed firearm?

Barber: Yes. I have to protect myself.

Me: It's amazing that you believe and speak so high about a "Protecting God", yet you carry a firearm for protection. You've asked me, "where's my faith?" I ask you, "Where's your faith?" Little do you know that you've just contradicted yourself and the belief in your "God of choice." Stick to cutting hair, it's what you do best. "God makes babies and fools, you've represented the fools extremely well...lol.

Owner: {says to barber} Damn, told you so!!

I pay, leave him a tip and walk out the door.

Again I say, "The biblical/ book deities NEVER looked out for ANYONE, NOT even their own in the stories..."

Let me PROVE IT, "He that spared not his own Son, but delivered him up for us all, how shall he not with him also freely give us all things? {Rom 8:32} KJV

In other words, "If he didn't spare his own, how in the hell is he going to spare you?"

"Faith, Hope and Belief" are DANGEROUS words that will keep people wondering.

"The Mega Church Pastor"

Me: Hello Sir! How are you

Pastor: Good afternoon Sir

Me: Very beautiful church.

Pastor: Why thank you. God is good!!

Me: You mean to tell me God actually tossed money bags out of heaven?

Pastor: {laughing} of course not!! I've been in full time ministry for thirty years. All I ever do is pray and thank the good Lord for providing. They have provided a church that seats 20,000 people at a time for three (3) services; a million dollar home; a private jet; food on the table and two (2) half a million dollar vehicles.

Me: Excuse me Sir, but you said, "They!"

Pastor: Yes! "They" meaning the people.

Me: So, the people are considered "God's?"

Pastor: Absolutely!! They have the power to make choices.

Me: Why do you preach about a "Jesus" if you consider them to be Gods?

Pastor: If the people are silly enough to believe in a person they'll never see, who am I to change their minds? I'm benefiting from their ignorance.

Me: Wouldn't it be easier to explain that God has given them the power within, instead of telling them to wait on the Lord?

Pastor: Hell no!! I'm going to milk the superficial product until their giving cease. Change and truth are two things that are hard for people to accept. If they've already received the lie, keeping giving it.

Me: Wouldn't they accept the truth if you taught it?

Pastor: Nope!! You can't give them what they're not ready for.

POINT: Religion taught people to denounce themselves the credit they rightfully deserve. Any leader will cash in on a person's ignorance at any given time. Learn to discern with your God given spirit and you'll always come out on top. - ***Lamont Bershawn***

EYE'VE STOOD INSIDE THE EYE OF HELL AND REMAINED FEARLESS!

"WAL-MART EMPLOYEE"

Cashier: That's a beautiful cross around your neck
Me: Thank you! However, it's not a cross it's an Ankh
Cashier: What's the difference?
Me: The Ankh is a symbol of life. The cross is a symbol of death.
Cashier: So, you don't believe in Jesus?
Me: Absolutely NOT!! I used to be a Pastor and would drill that nonsense into folks mind concerning a mythical Savior.
Cashier: Well, who or what do you worship?
Me: I worship myself, nature and humanity.
Cashier: Anyone that refuses to worship my Lord and Savior Jesus Christ is voided from my life.
Me: You chose to engage in this conversation with me. I just wanted to purchase these items. You said, "Anyone refusing to worship your Lord and Savior is voided from your life." Do you have a Face book page?
Cashier: Yes, I do.
Me: When you get a chance make sure you delete it because Mark Zuckerberg doesn't worship your Savior neither.

As a matter of FACT, you may as well clock out because your employer refuses to worship your Savior too, here at Wal-Mart.

Cashier: What do you mean?
Me: You began to judge me because I don't worship who you worship, or believe in who you choose to believe in; but you're employed by a Corporation that worships humanity. I'm sure your boss isn't waiting on your Jesus to bless him, because they have the products that consumers need/ want. Jesus can't to a damn thing for them.
Cashier: I never looked at it like that.
Me: It was a pleasure having this conversation with you. Be sure to go to Amazon.com and get the book, "Bishops Need Love Too."

{As I walked away one of her co-workers smiled at me and said, "She always get into religious conversations with people. I'm glad you set her straight."}

Me: I respect everyone's belief. I just expect people to respect mine too. I don't claim to know it all. I just know my personal experiences and what they've taught me.

POINT: Regardless of anyone's belief system. You have your personal experiences that you can't deny. They're not written in any book, but have become branded as a trial in your life. You go through things in order to learn from them, NOT for them to become repetitive. - **Lamont Bershawn**

"The Depressed Man"

Men/ Fathers: Never disrespect your wife in front of your children, especially your male children. Seeing this, they'll begin to feel its okay for them to disrespect their own mother and other women.

Why? Children go by the things they visualize as well as hear. This is why actions speak louder than words.

When a child sees their mother being abused {physically, psychologically, verbally}, children take on those actions. Remember, what a child see/view is often what they'll accept as the correct form of teaching.

I had a conversation with a man that didn't want to accept that he was disrespecting his wife on many accounts or he just refused to comprehend what he was doing was considered abuse. Honestly, it seemed he had more respect for others opposed to his immediate family.

During the conversation I asked, "Where's your son?" He responded, "He's incarcerated. He was framed for murder and received a life sentence." I asked, "Was he married?" "Yes", he replied as he began shaking his head in sorrow. "What's wrong?", I asked.

He responded:

EYE'VE STOOD INSIDE THE EYE OF HELL AND REMAINED FEARLESS!

"It's all my fault. He saw me mistreat his mother; so when he got married he began mistreating his wife. He knew that I consistently stepped out on his mother and my son did the same to his wife. The only difference between my son and I is that I never brought my trash home. My son put his wife out and brought the trash to live in with him. In the end, instead of my son getting rid of the trash; the trash ended up burning him. Now, when I visit my son I can only see myself in him."

POINT: Just because you got away with something, doesn't mean that those who consider you a mentor that follow in your footsteps will get away with the same thing. Children pay attention to the very thing, you're thinking they're not even considering. Keep in mind; people are watching you, when you're thinking that things are going unnoticed!! – **Lamont Bershawn**

"THE ANGEL IN DISGUISE"

I went to the grocery store yesterday so I could grab a few items for my trip today. I saw a good friend of mine's in one of the aisles and we engaged in a conversation. She was telling me that she read my book, "Bishops Need Love Too" and how most of what I wrote about resonated with her spirit. As we stood there talking about the church, religion, scripture vs. spirituality; people were being drawn.

An older lady, approx. 80 yrs. old, looked at me as I began explaining things that I wrote in my book and said, "Young man, I admire your teachings. I didn't want to interfere with your conversation but it was music to my ears. I lived in the church and followed the bible, but caught more hell in my three (3) marriages because I denied my heart only to conform to religion. Please write down the information about your book, so I can tell my grandson to get it." {She walks away smiling}.

My friend begins to tell me how she neglected, disregarded and denounced her gifts because the church leaders told her that: (1) it was a sin to contact deceased spirits (2) she shouldn't open portals to entertain "unknown" spirits (3) she would be denied by "God" if she wouldn't surrender to the "word of God"/ bible.

{A little background on my friend} Very spiritual, business minded person. Went through a few hardships that destroyed her livelihood, separated her family and she ended up homeless. Prior to the homelessness, she was a real life medium {person that's able to speak with/ see the deceased}. I personally tested her clairvoyance as we were on the phone about something she had no knowledge about. VERY ACCURATE!! She NEVER asked for money, although people would give her donations. I'm not speaking of a prophet that will "profit-lie" for monetary gain.

She began to cry and say, "The more I tune into the church, the more I feel myself fading away. It's like I'm trying to give God my all, but I'm suffering in the midst. I've prayed, fasted, tarried, have learned to speak in unknown tongues, etc. Name it, I've done it; yet I'm still holding on. What more can I do?"

An older man came over and handed her his handkerchief. He introduced himself to us. He said, "Hello! My name is Shem and I come in peace." He asked her, "Are you a Christian?" She said, "yes."

So, the church leaders told you: (1) it was a sin to contact deceased spirits (2) she shouldn't open portals to entertain "unknown" spirits (3) she would be denied by "God" if she wouldn't surrender to the "word of God"/ bible? She responded, "yes."

{What he said next flipped me out}!! "How could the church leaders say that to you, yet they're either calling upon/ worshiping someone that's deceased or never existed named {Jesus}?"

"Keep teaching young man, you're on the path of greatness and your work is being noticed", he replied.

{The next gesture blew me away}: He handed her an envelope and said, "This is for you!" When she opened the envelope Shem was gone. The look on her face was as if she'd just seen a ghost. I asked, "What's wrong?" She pulled out ten crisp $100.00 bills.

I was awaiting the norm, "Thank you Jesus"; but she didn't speak those words. However, she thanked the spirit that was in tuned with her spirit all along. It showed up to let her know "IT" hadn't forgotten about her.

EYE'VE STOOD INSIDE THE EYE OF HELL AND REMAINED FEARLESS!

POINT/ MESSAGE: Don't ever allow church leaders, family or those "frienemies" to make YOU deny YOUR truth for something that's COUNTERFEIT!! – *Lamont Bershawn*

"THE EVANGELIST"

A few months ago I received a call from an "Evangelist" who just graduated "Evangelism school/ school of Evangelism." She started the conversation as general as she could have by asking me about the well being of my family.

She said, "The Lord placed you inside of my spirit and had me contact you." I responded, "What exactly did the Lord want you to tell me that he, she or it couldn't have told me themselves?"

She said, "I had a dream that you were at a church or some sort of coliseum preaching to millions of people. You were wearing your black cassock {robe}; in an instant the ceiling of the church opened up and the hand of God killed you for leading the people against the word of God."

Eye asked, "Are you sure the message or dream was for me?"

{Laughing hysterically} Eye said, "The only part of your dream that was about me was that you saw me leading the people out of bondage into knowing that they are the manuscripts of God. In other words, I'm leading them into understanding who in FACT are the AUTHENTIC words of God. I'm leading them against the bullshit that's being taught inside of the churches that are keeping them enslaved and leading them into their personal created HELL."

I went on to say, "Allow me to dissect your dream with all accuracy. I was the one in the coliseum {many churches combined} with the message by God to FREE the minds of the people with TRUTH.

It was actually you wearing the black robe because God knew you're standing inside of the pulpits as the (1) whore of Babylon chasing one man that won't pay you any attention (2) screwing the man's best friend to cause conflict (3) church gossiper (4) getting involved with other folks relationships/ marriages telling the "testimonial" secrets to one another (5) telling lies on people to make yourself feel good knowing you're miserable as hell, etc.

The black robe represented the darkness that you've created that your life was spiraling into." Now look at you, you can't hardly walk, you're a beggar, have no friends and your family members don't want to deal with you.

"When you saw the hand coming out of the ceiling, it was the sign to you that you don't have long to get your life together."

{The phone was quiet for approx. 45 seconds} I said, "Are you still there?"

She responded {in tears}, "I receive it. How can I make things right? I've done so much wrong to the point that no one wants to be bothered with me."

I kindly responded, "You've conformed so much to the church and your religious beliefs to the point you lost self in the process of trying to find God. It's not too late to make amends." She responded, "I want to apologize to you."

POINT: Just because someone deep inside of the church tells you a "Dream" or "Prophesy" over you doesn't mean it's meant for you. God/ Jesus/ Lord have no reason to go through ANYONE to get YOUR attention. STOP accepting other folk's dreams and claiming them as yours! – **Lamont Bershawn**

"THE COOKOUT"

Over the weekend a friend of mine called me and invited me to a cookout. I really didn't have any plans so I accepted the invitation. When I arrived, there were plenty of people eating, playing all sorts of card games {bid whist, spades, tonk and pinochle}, playing volleyball and even horse shoes.

You know there were the usual groups talking about politics and religion. I didn't engage in any of the discussions as I sat back and enjoyed the great food.

EYE'VE STOOD INSIDE THE EYE OF HELL AND REMAINED FEARLESS!

One of the teenagers engaged in the religious conversation. He said, "Can I ask a question?" One of the gentleman said, "What is your question young man?"

When I was in elementary school I remember having to come home and study for spelling tests, math tests, science tests, etc. just to test my knowledge on those particular subjects.

When do we get the test after we leave bible study?

I mean, isn't there a test that we must take to test our knowledge according to the subject at hand?

The people stood silent for a few moments until his father said, "Our faith is tested daily as we continue to live our lives." The teenager replied, "Is that why people remain in the same church for many years under the same preacher, yet don't graduate or excel to the next level?"

Is this why we simultaneously go to church to be on one accord with everyone else?

Have any of you ever taken the time to really evaluate why we're constantly going to a church going through the rituals, saying the prayers, giving the money to a "God/ Jesus" we never see for a blessing we'll never get?

{Pastor/ person that blessed the food steps in}

"Young man, this is why we must live by faith. You know faith is the substance of things hoped for, the evidence of things not seen."

{Teenager} "Dad, may I respond?" "Most certainly son", replied the teens dad.

"Well, you're not living by faith preacher because you know what's coming into the ministry every week and can live according as such. It's the people that don't know where their next meal is coming from, how they're going to make ends meet without two nickels to rub together and the one's giving their last in the offering plate that's living by faith.

You see the job of a real leader is to lead/ guide the flock, NOT tell their sheep to jump into something they're not willing to jump into themselves."

{Look on Pastor's face ---------> PRICELESS!!}!!

Lady at the table yells, "I got next on the card table!!" {As she gets up from the table of religious conversation}.

POINT: Older folk can learn a lot from a younger person, if they're willing to listen!! – **Lamont Bershawn**

"An Eye Opener"

I went to Wal-Mart the other day to pick up a few things for my fishing tackle box along with a few items to take hunting. As I headed to the cashier I realized that I needed a few more items, so I picked them up too.

When I approached the cashier to pay for my items, an older woman who was behind me said, "Excuse me young man. Don't take this the wrong way but are you a preacher?" I responded, "I used to be." She said, "What do you mean used to be?" I smiled and said, "It's a long story ma'am." {As I handed her the business card with "Bishops Need Love Too" information on it.}. She looked at the card and said, "Very interesting title of the book."

As I headed out of Wal-Mart, the lady wasn't too far behind me. I looked back {smiling} and said, "Don't forget to purchase the book. I promise you won't be able to put it down." The lady looked at me and asked, "Have you eaten yet? There's a nice Chinese buffet a few blocks away, meet me there.

I have a few questions and I feel you're the correct person to talk with. I'm sorry, I didn't ask if you were available for a mid day conversation." {I can't lie as the first thing crossing my mind was "How Stella Got Her Groove Back" along with the character "Barbie" from my book.}. I replied, "I'll meet you there."

When we met at the restaurant, we introduced ourselves to each other. We sat down as we began to chat and chew.

She stated, "I was raised in a Christian family. My parents attended a Pentecostal church and that's what my beliefs were grounded/ molded under.

EYE'VE STOOD INSIDE THE EYE OF HELL AND REMAINED FEARLESS!

In 1973, at the age of 23, I married my high school sweetheart. We attended the same church for many years until we realized the Pastor was receiving money for a building fund for ten years and no ground breaking ceremony had taken place, yet the Pastor had a brand new car every two years."

My question to you is, "Why are church leaders, especially in the black church preaching about a Jesus that can do so much, but he couldn't save his own ass?"

{My mouth hit the floor as I had no idea this would be the types of questions she had}.

I responded, "Jesus has been a money making name and product for many years. People are led into fear based theologies for centuries. These scare tactics have been passed through the generations and have cursed people preventing them from using logic in order to conform to religious doctrine.

To be honest, many people are afraid to deal with the reality of SELF, the reality of who they really are because they don't like the person they've become. In order NOT to deal with their reality, they create a fantasy in order to suppress who they are and what they see.

A preacher MUST teach according to the guidelines of their organization, if they desire to maintain a position in that church. Preachers are like drug dealers, they're in it to be the person in "Charge." They'll sell their drug to anyone willing to buy it. The difference is that a drug dealer knows what they're distributing while the preacher have no clue, all they know is people come daily to get the drug they consistently call "The Word."

The lady, who is every bit of 65 replied, "Wow, I've never heard a preacher say that." I replied, "You probably never will. That's why I said I used to be a preacher. I left the church, lost a lot of friends/colleagues, been slandered all because I made a decision NOT to continue enslaving the people."

The lady looked at me {smiling} and said, "I've been an Atheist for the last 15 years and I knew my spirit wasn't leading me away from the church in error. God placed me in line behind you for a reason and I'm very grateful for it. You just sold another book because I'm purchasing my copy as soon as I get home."

I responded, "You just said God placed you behind me for a reason. I thought Atheists didn't believe in God?" She smiled and said, "We don't!" {As she treated me to the lunch}.

POINT: People are creatures of habit that must feel the need to be a part of something in order to function properly. What/ Who "God" is to one may NOT be to another. A label or title will never be able to properly define anything. Learn to look beyond or within the label/ title to see the authenticity of the object/ product. – **Lamont Bershawn**

"This is Your Conscience"

In case you're wondering what/ who I am? I am the awareness of a moral or ethical aspect to your conduct together with the urge to prefer right over wrong. I am the part of the superego in psychoanalysis that judges the ethical nature of your actions and thoughts and then transmits such determinations to your ego for consideration.

I am the place that house the information from Most High, Supreme Architect, God, etc. that takes PRECEDENCE over any book or resource because I am connected to the SOURCE that controls YOU!!

Many of you have questioned me from time to time and ultimately went against me by relying on something you read that didn't even concern you, but you thought that it was needed information. You began to store it within your brain and it became a constant battle, struggle and fight. Why? It's because you read it and stored the information that totally contradicted the most powerful source that will guide you to success. This is your conscience!!

Many of you have neglected me because of (1) peer pressure (2) a rough situation (3) negative circumstance (4) "Physically Visually Impaired" {you witnessed or actually saw the incident, but misread/ misinterpreted the actual event}

(5) "Dedicated Ignorance" {When you know something isn't right but by CHOICE you remain and learn/ embed the material

EYE'VE STOOD INSIDE THE EYE OF HELL AND REMAINED FEARLESS!

as concrete or absolute} (6) sexual advances {deep down within me, you KNEW you didn't want it but gave it a thought and ended up regretting it - LET'S BE REAL!!}!!

This is your conscience!!

Allow me to go DEEPER:

You see the enemy is always on the attack. If the enemy can't get to the Head {Brain}, the attack now becomes physical. It causes turmoil wherever it possibly can. This is when I {your conscience} steps in letting the enemy know "That no weapon formed against YOU shall prosper."

You see, what the enemy is so confused about is that it tried everything in its power to kill you because it sees what you're bound to become. What the enemy didn't realize was that every time you went to church to hear a sermon, every time you became emotional by listening to gospel music, every time you listened to someone else's testimony {that may have sounded like a similar situation}, every time you prayed {still waiting on an answer}, the enemy didn't get a response. When it threw that very thing that once had you bound and still there was NO REACTION, it didn't recognize that it was no longer living, but now DEAD!!

This is your conscience!!

Your flesh becomes confused and begins to have a conversation with your spirit!!

Flesh: Why didn't you tell me?
Spirit: If I would have told you, we would have never gotten delivered
Flesh: I didn't want to be delivered
Spirit: I realized that...lol. That's the reason why I was connected to your conscience all along and was preparing for battle.
Conscience: {laughing at flesh} I told you never to bring a knife to a gun fight!!
Don't you know I am the part of the "I AM?" I must remain covered and protected at all times. Remember this while you're resting, "I NEVER Sleep!!"
THIS IS YOUR CONSCIENCE!! – *Lamont Bershawn*

LAMONT BERSHAWN

"The Word Became Flesh"

A Bishop in boxed me and asked me to explain the Biblical chapter and verses of John 1:1, "In the beginning was the Word, and the Word was with God, and the Word was God."

John 1:14, "And the Word was made flesh, and dwelt among us, (and we beheld his glory, the glory as of the only begotten of the Father,) full of grace and truth."

The Bishop told me that this is how God became Jesus {in the flesh} and was perfect walking/ living in Earth among the people.

My response to this Bishop:

When we look at the beginning of anything, it begins/ starts with a thought, a dream or something that's envisioned. This is the "Word" that have come from within YOUR very being. So you're now the CREATOR of THAT "Word/ phrase" that have come from within and is now WITH you.

The "Word/ phrase" cannot become "God" UNTIL the "Word/ phrase" BECOMES a REALITY. When the "Word" that you've thought or envisioned BECOMES a REALITY, then it BECOMES a part of YOUR FLESH because YOU'RE NOW in the PROCESS of Living out YOUR DREAM!!

Here's an example:

You're a child and have a dream, vision or a desire to be on T.V. {this is the WORD that came from within YOU}. You write the dream on a piece of paper {Now the words are WITH you because you've made them plain and visual}.

You awaken every morning to look at what you wrote down and put every effort to make YOUR dream come true. Twenty- five years later YOU catch a big break and YOUR opportunity to be on T.V. has arrived {Now YOUR PERSONAL words/ phrase have become YOUR REALITY, which is what YOU placed in your atmosphere and is a part of YOU. By SPEAKING it into existence made it YOUR REALITY and became a part of YOUR FLESH because it came from WITHIN YOUR SPIRIT}.

God was NOT "Jesus" in the FLESH, nor was "Jesus" perfect!!

EYE'VE STOOD INSIDE THE EYE OF HELL AND REMAINED FEARLESS!

Everyone has their OWN EXPERIENCES with God, NOT to be based off "Jesus" experience or the following of a book.

Look at it like this:

Everyone have different goals. There's some that want follow in their parents footsteps which is perfectly fine "IF" that's where your SPIRIT, PASSION or HEART is.

POINT: YOUR destiny BEGINS from a THOUGHT birthed by YOUR God from WITHIN YOUR spirit. This is EXACTLY why I CONSTANTLY say, "God is a PERSONAL Concept that people have made a COLLECTIVE REALITY."

Everyone have a DIFFERENT mindset, level of THINKING, upbringing/ raising and EXPERIENCE in life which will ALWAYS be GUIDED by YOUR PERSONAL God!!

Remember, someone else's ambitions and goals will NEVER work for YOU because they weren't BIRTHED within YOU.

YOUR LIFE is NOT to be COMPARED to the Bible because YOU'RE NOT the AUTHOR/ CREATOR of ANY of the BOOKS that were COMPILED in it!! – **Lamont Bershawn**

"Leaving the Pulpit for Good"

I can recall my last few years being in the pulpit either writing or preaching a sermon. My spirit and my flesh were constantly in a battle. My spirit no longer wanted to continue to be a part of the "circus" because I was the narrator/ orator and people listened to the bullshit I'd spew from the bible {bye-bull}.

I knew people would listen because 40% were seeking answers outside of themselves because of a bad decision they made; 50% continued following because they didn't want to disappoint their parents, even though they felt it was some shit in the game; 10% really had no comprehension skills whatsoever.

I refuse to lie and say that it wasn't pleasing to my flesh at times or beneficial. I enjoyed being treated like I was part of the "Royal Priesthood or family." Yes, I was great at selling the false product known as "Jesus."

I remember receiving a call from a female Pastor that asked for my help to assist her in finding scripture for a theme for her occasion. She just couldn't seem to find what she needed to make sense. I helped her and she was so excited that she couldn't wait until her service the next day. I remember hanging up the phone and preparing my own sermon. The topic of the sermon was, "Eye Refuse to be Bound!"

The next morning when I awakened I knew this would be my final curtain call. Evidently, not because I would physically perish but being defined by religion was going to be dead to me. Don't get me wrong or misinterpret why I still occasionally get involved into heated debates. It's NOT because I'm trying to prove my point, but to help others see what really have them walking by "faith" or being blinded by.

When I entered the pulpit that morning I began to have a conversation with "THE LIVING GOD."

GOD:
EYE'VE BEEN PREPARING YOU FOR SUCH A TIME AS THIS. EYE DIDN'T BRING YOU THIS FAR TO LEAVE YOU. THIS MESSAGE WILL CATAPULT YOU INTO A HIGHER DIMENSION THAT WILL RING OUTSIDE THE WALLS OF THIS INSTITUTION.

Me: Why did EYE remain so long?

GOD:
EYE KEPT YOU IN IT SO THAT YOU COULD FULLY UNDERSTAND AND MADE AWARE OF WHOM THE REAL GOD WAS. IT WOULD'VE BEEN HARD FOR YOU TO SEE DUE TO THE STRONGHOLDS THAT WERE OVER YOU. IT'S IMPERATIVE FOR ME TO FINALLY BRING YOU OUT OF THIS SHIT SO THAT PEOPLE CAN GET A GLIMPSE OF THE REAL YOU.
YOU SEE THE DIFFERENCE IS THAT YOU REALLY LOVE TO HELP PEOPLE, NOT FEED THEM THE LIES FOR YOUR PERSONAL GAIN, NOT PISS ON THEM AND TELL THEM IT'S RAINING.

EYE'VE STOOD INSIDE THE EYE OF HELL AND REMAINED FEARLESS!

Me: Let's not prolong this. Eye'm ready!!
{SERMON DELIVERED}!!
{Walking out of the church receiving hugs, handshakes and kisses on the cheek}.
Eye get outside of the doors feeling relieved or as if a ton of bricks lifted off of me.
There were three familiar folks standing outside awaiting my arrival with tears in their eyes.
Me: Why were you three outside waiting for me instead of being a part of the service?
GOD:
THAT'S A PLACE FOR THOSE THAT DON'T KNOW WHO THEY ARE OR THE POWER THEY REALLY POSSESS!!
Little did Eye know when Eye walked out of the church for the "Last Hurrah" my spirit, my conscience and MY GOD {GUIDE} would be waiting for me.

POINT: DON'T EVER GET TO A POINT IN LIFE THAT YOU LOSE YOURSELF, YOUR IDENTITY OR YOUR DIGNITY IN ANYTHING THAT'S REALLY NOT BENEFICIAL FOR YOU OR ANYONE ELSE!! – **Lamont Bershawn**

"FORNICATION"

And the voice of God came upon me saying, "I want u to go and find a virgin. When you find her, I want u to fuck her and when u fuck her I want u to impregnate her. In 9 mos. she's going to birth a set of male twins and their names shall be Pete and Repeat."

Me: You want me to engage in "fornication?" Isn't it written that it's better to marry than burn?
God: I had nothing to do with that book or the conversations in that book. I'm too powerful, too discreet to come and cause worldly confusion. The book you're speaking of was that of a little "God" called manipulation.

Me: You mean the words in the Bible are NOT your words? Why do so many people call it or consider it the "Word of God?"
God: It's because many people have totally missed out on these personal conversations because they'd rather tune into, tap into, or believe that which can be read, written and altered. Remember, I am the I AM and I don't need a mediator or any type of device to connect with my people.
Me: What should I tell the people?
God: Tell them to put the books down and begin to feel me with their hearts. Open their ears to be able to accept what I give them. The books have clouded their true sense of who I am. When they have heard me correctly, they'll be no more hate, no more confusion and no more devastation upon the land.

My love covers the entire multitude!!! - **Lamont Bershawn**

No Mediator Needed"

And the voice of the MOST HIGH came upon me saying,
"TELL THE PEOPLE THAT WHEN THEY CALL UPON THE NAME OF JESUS AND THEY DON'T GET A RESPONSE, IT'S BECAUSE I HAVE EQUIPPED MY PEOPLE WITH THEIR NECESSITIES PRIOR TO ALLOWING THEM TO ENTER INTO THE WORLD. {NO MEDIATOR NEEDED}

JESUS WAS SENT FOR THOSE INDIVIDUALS WHO COULDN'T GRASP HOLD OF REALITY AND NEEDED TO READ ABOUT A FIGURE TO ENLIGHTEN, EMPOWER, ENCOURAGE, AND EDUCATE THEM.

I HAVE EQUALLY CREATED EVERY INDIVIDUAL WITHOUT CAUSING DIVISION. I HAVE NOT PLACED ANY BOOK IN MY PLACE TO INTOXICATE THE POTENTIAL LEVEL OF YOUR THOUGHT.

WITHIN EACH OF YOU ARE THE KEYS AND ANSWERS TO A SUCCESSFUL LIFE.

*EYE'VE STOOD INSIDE THE EYE OF HELL
AND REMAINED FEARLESS!*

STOP ALLOWING DEVICES AND DECOYS TO ALLOW YOU TO DEVIATE OR DISTRACT YOU; CAUSING DIVISION IN ORDER TO SET YOU UP FOR DESTRUCTION!"

I HAVE SPOKEN!! {Voice of The Most High} – **Lamont Bershawn**

"In The Womb"

A very long time ago while being inside my mother's womb I envisioned a throne fit for a King. I stood up and began to inspect my surroundings. As I walked around I saw many beings that I never knew, but as I passed them they saluted me and stood at attention. I respectfully nodded my head to acknowledge everyone that I saw.

Out from the left a voice spoke to me {while kneeling} and said, "Hello Sir! They call me Adversary. I'm the one you've chosen to cause enough conflict during your earthly tenure in order to keep you on the right track." I responded, "Arise Adversary, this is a journey that neither you nor I will ever forget."

As I walked a little further to the right of me stepped out a set of triplets. They spoke in unison {while kneeling} and said, "Hello Sir! Our names are Trials, Tribulation and Temptation. We're the ones that you've chosen that will be in other people's paths that you'll come in contact with; the ones that will be there during your sleepless nights; the ones that will cause so much doubt. I responded, "Arise my set of triplets, this is a journey that neither you nor I will ever forget."

As I looked above my head, there were a set of twins hovering over my head. I asked, "Who might you be?" They said, "Your Excellency, we are Crown and Conqueror. We shall hover over you from now until eternity as you continue to rise above the feats of life."

Confused as all get out, I approached the throne and asked, "Where is the owner of this throne?"

In an instant, everyone knelt as the mirrors stood at attention speaking, "You are the Owner, Creator and King!"

POINT: While you yet were inside of the Goddess womb, you were the heir to the throne of life {glory}. You chose every battle/ fight, temptation/ trial and conflicting source. In other words, you knew them prior to your earthly existence.

Have you forgotten who you are? Have you really demoted your REAL name for a makeshift title?

Go back to the beginning and reclaim all that you've sold, was stolen or relinquished. It's all in the wrong hands/ possession if it's NOT in YOURS!! – **Lamont Bershawn**

"THE BATTLE OF THE GODS"

And the voice of God came unto me unto me and said, "I WANT YOU TO GATHER ALL OF THE OTHER GODS SO WE CAN DETERMINE WHO'S ACTUALLY THE MOST POWERFUL OF THEM ALL."

I began sending emails, text messages, prayers, tarrying, smoke signals and chants just to see which "Gods" would show. To my surprise a few of them showed up. Being seated in my presence was (1) the Biblical God (2) the "God" of ignorance (3) Mammon (4) Alcoholism (5) Drug addiction (6) Sexual addictions, etc.

The "Biblical" God responded with such force, "This is a no brainer. Don't you see that I've conquered a majority of the world? I have them mesmerized by my words."

"I beg to differ" said, Mammon. Don't you know I have people stealing, killing/ murdering and telling lies because of me?

Alcoholism responded, "I'm going to remove myself because I'm just a temporary fix that people tend to lean upon and get emotional."

Drug addiction put its two cents in to say, "Once a person hits me I'll have them in the palm of my hands begging for me."

Sex addiction hollered out, "Hold up one damn second. I have people turning tricks, getting all types of diseases, destroying relationships/ marriages and the prime concern on these talk shows. Just look at Jerry Springer and Maury."

The "God" of ignorance laughed aloud and said, "I'm presented as truth and will continue to prey on the weak minded as long as they continue to allow the blind to lead them, allow the deaf to guide them and allow the dumb to speak to them."

As they were speaking among themselves, the room began to tremble with a thunderous sound as the "Voice" entered into the room laughing. The "Voice" responded to each of the other "gods."

"Biblical" God? How is it that you're the most powerful when your words couldn't put an end to slavery? BE GONE!!

"Mammon?" The greatest things on this planet have no use for you, they're PRICELESS!! BE GONE!!

"Alcoholism, Drug addiction, Sexual addiction?" {Before the "Voice" could respond they vanished}.

"Looks like it's between you {God of Ignorance} and me" said, the Voice.

The God of Ignorance stated, "You're powerful to those that knows how to tap into their own spirits to hear your VOICE, but I'm just as powerful to those that tap into their own spirits but REFUSE to take heed and therefore makes the decision to DENY truth. As the "Voice" began walking around the room full of mirrors it recognized, it was speaking with itself the entire time.

POINT: The true battle is the battle that takes place within SELF!! – **Lamont Bershawn.**

"Conversation with Mother"

It's been about thirteen years since my mother had any problems or serious pain in her body. I was at the house later that evening because we were supposed to be going to the casino, but around midnight she asked me to take her to the emergency room. When she got ready we were on our way; we arrived at the hospital around one o'clock in the morning. I sat in the waiting room as she was called back so she could get checked out by the doctor. I began dosing off, so I went to my car and turned it on so it could get warm and fell asleep. Little did I know I slept longer than I expected. I shut down the car and went back inside of the emergency room. When the receptionist let me in the back to see her, the doctor just finished running tests.

I asked my mother, "What did the doctor say?" She responded, "The doctor said the cancer returned on my pancreas." My heart dropped as if I just received a death sentence for something I didn't do.

Me: Mom are you afraid of dying?
Mom: No. God answered my prayers. I wanted to see my children grown and on their own. I got to see my grandchildren become adults and had the opportunity to see my first grandchild married with her first baby. The prayer that hasn't been answered thus far is my oldest child is still physically incarcerated.
Me: What if I told you that you were able to see all of that come to pass was because of your will to do so and not your prayers? Do you remember you asked me to pray for you because you believed that God worked through me? Well, you were healed by a few things (1) Your will to be healed (2) My will for you to live. The most powerful source we have is our will because it remains connected to the Living God.
There's a bible verse which becomes confusing to people, "Where two or three are gathered together in my name, I'll be there in the midst." What that actually means is that when two minds are in agreement for a specific purpose or concern with positive energy; whatever our desire is it must happen. It's like summoning something to happen. You were the first God that Eye ever knew, but through your religious belief you introduced me to a powerless, created God.
Mom: You know you have a way with words that make people really think hard about what they believe?
Me: I've heard that before. You have to understand that I was a Pastor and preached for years, until the Living God told me to leave. God asked me, "Am I going to continue enslaving the people or will Eye begin enlightening them?" The choice became extremely easy after Eye became sick and tired of seeing peo-

EYE'VE STOOD INSIDE THE EYE OF HELL AND REMAINED FEARLESS!

ple broke, busted and disgusted coming to the church for relief they'd never receive. Eye love you and don't ever want anything to happen to you, especially if Eye know you have the power within instead of waiting on a biblical deity.

Often times we fall short waiting on things to answer us when all we have to do is realize who is in power over self.

Mom: Well, people have been calling and praying for me showing their concern and I appreciate them for it.
Me: Eye appreciate them too because it shows you who cares about you. Eye no longer subscribe or solicit anyone's prayer because for one it doesn't work and everyone's heart isn't in the right place concerning you. Nevertheless, we both know you're going to be ok.
Mom: I love you Lamont.
Me: Eye love you too mom.

BE·TRAY·AL

[bə'trāəl, bē'trāəl]
NOUN
The action of betraying one's country, a group, or a person; treachery.

IT'S SAD TO SAY BUT in this day and time we must be careful of the people we associate with, confide in, joke with, consider a best friend, your very own family members and even the individual you're dating or married to. Eye'll say in any case or matter, "Don't ever take it to a court of public opinion, a municipal court, social media or any court where there's a judge or jury present because you'll never win or be vindicated."

In EVERY form/ aspect of business there's a pawn. A pawn is one willing to make a sacrifice

(1) because shit isn't going on with them or in their life, so in turn they'll do their best to destroy YOU in order to gain notoriety (2) a jealous/ envious and cunning "mutha fukka" that lurks around YOU, watching YOUR every move in order to try to take over YOUR position/ status.

NOTE: THERE'S A PAWN IN YOUR CAMP AS YOU'RE READING THIS POST!!!

EYE'VE STOOD INSIDE THE EYE OF HELL AND REMAINED FEARLESS!

Allow me to break this down because most of you have either played or learned the game of checkers, but never took the time to learn chess.

When engaging with social media or media in general, you better learn the game of chess. In checkers you're allowed to single jump, double jump, but can't jump backwards until you become the "King."

In Chess:

Pawns can only move forward. On their first move, they can move one or two squares. Afterwards, they can move only one square at a time. They can capture an enemy piece by moving one square forward diagonally.

Bishops can move any number of squares diagonally.

Knights can move only in an L-shape, one square up and two over, or two squares over and one down, or any such combination of one-two or two-one movements in any direction.

Rooks can move any number of squares, up and down and side to side.

Queens can move any number of squares along ranks, files and diagonals.

Kings can move one square at a time in any direction.

"OUR" focus is the pawn. Do you see how the pawn is the only "mutha fukka" that can change directions?

Church folk: Remember how Bishop Paul Morton lost everything in Hurricane Katrina? How he had to rebuild after losing three (3) "Mega Churches?" He moved to Atlanta and immediately built a Mega Church. When the controversy concerning Bishop Eddie Long aired, Bishop Morton publicly called him out for an apology. This was Morton's opportune time to try his best to get some of Eddie Longs members. Yes, the church is a cutthroat business where many snakes and wolves reside.

NOTE: EYE DON'T CONDONE ANY OF THE ALLEGATIONS BROUGHT FORTH CONCERNING EDDIE LONG. I'M JUST TRYING TO MAKE A POINT!!

Has ANYONE ever heard of Hannibal Buress? FUCK NO!!

He's being called the "hero" {by some} that ignited the downfall of Bill Cosby. By others he's being blackballed and known as "the nigga that you better not trust." Again, NOT condoning any of the allegations brought forth concerning Mr. Cosby.

If you're wondering why Eye haven't posted everyday like Eye used to in the previous years? It's because Eye know there's a few snakes and wolves waiting their opportune time to infiltrate what Eye've got going.

NOTE: PEOPLE WILL BELIEVE A LIE QUICKER THAN THEY'LL RECEIVE THE TRUTH!! IF YOU DON'T KNOW IT TO BE FACTUAL, JUST LOOK AT WHAT RELIGION HAS DONE AND IS STILL DOING TO PEOPLE!!

Be watchful concerning ANY form of media {PEOPLE, FACEBOOK, MYSPACE, TWITTER, PERISCOPE, INSTAGRAM, ETC}. They'll build you up in order to set you up for the greatest downfall of your life.

Through life experience learning to trust people is the hardest thing for people to do, especially if one has been betrayed. In my assessment of living, there's no such thing as a "confidant", best friend or family member that won't betray you. It took me awhile to understand this, but in the bible where "Jesus" is speaking saying, "I'll stick closer than any brother..." My first question would be, "Why would Eye trust a total stranger?" Eye understand what that particular passage means now. The scripture was eluding to the point that everyone will eventually let you down, disappoint you or have a motive to betray you. Eye must admit that Eye totally agree with the way the mobsters/ mafia define family or "familia." The way they choose a brother is by actually cutting each other's finger and touching blood to blood or using a sharp knife using the pointed blade and pricking a little hole in each other's fingers and touching blood to blood. All of it signifies that we're blood brothers and we now have one another's backs and best interests. It doesn't matter if we weren't birthed by the same mother.

> *"BETRAYAL is the worst fucking sin; especially by those you once considered kin!"- Alexander Hardy*

In my adult life Eye've learned to choose my friends, "frienemies" {those individuals that act as a friend, but either have a motive for hanging around you or trying to infiltrate the positive things you have going on in your life} and those Eye allow to remain in my presence. Trust me, this isn't limited to outsiders but those that were born into the same bloodline, women that desired to be your significant other but were rejected for whatever reason, those women that actually became the significant other and even those people you allowed to experience the fruit from the blessings bestowed upon you.

In June, 2013, my very first book, "Bishops Need Love Too" was released under my pen name, Shannon Dougherty. The book was true to form and the pen name was used under the guidance of my publishers to prevent legal action. Eye recall a young lady reaching out to me on social media. She said that she's been a "follower" of mine and have been reading my posts daily. She said that she'd purchased my book and if Eye'm ever in the Atlanta area to let her know because she'd love for me to autograph her book and briefly converse with me. We'd been corresponding since that moment and she was always commenting on one of my controversial posts, some that which exceeded 800 {eight-hundred} comments. A few months later Eye was in the Atlanta area visiting my friend who just purchased his new home and was having a house warming party. Eye didn't invite her to the house warming party because Eye didn't know her like that and wouldn't invite a stranger to the place Eye was staying. Eye in boxed her and let her know that Eye was in town and we decided to meet at the food court in the shopping mall. We expressed to each other what we'd be wearing. Eye was casually dressed, wearing a pair of jeans and a buttoned shirt. She was wearing a pair of blue jeans, a pink blouse and a black leather vest. At first glance as Eye approached her she was all smiles as if we'd known each other for years. She greeted me with a hug and officially introduced herself.

Hello! My name is Alicia. Hello Alicia, Eye'm Lamont, it's a pleasure and honor to meet you. She responded, "the pleasures all mine." We began sitting at a table where she pulled out her book and Eye autographed it. Eye asked her what was it about the book that was most interesting to her? She replied, "She was a recovering Christian turned Atheist." Eye responded, "A recovering Christian?" Were you raised in the Christian faith, lost direction or hope and found it again, Eye'm confused. She smiled and said, "No, my mother raised me as a Christian but I no longer believe that mess." She went on and on about her personal experience and a few things that bothered her concerning the church. She went on to say that she's an Atheist and no longer believed in a God. Eye had to ask, "how did my book help you?" She replied, "you were so open about your journey from the pew to the pulpit and your personal experiences with church people, the thieves holding titles, the misinformation concerning the bible and the mass manipulation within the church."

She said, "I'm enjoying this conversation so much that I almost forgot that I must pick up my granddaughter." Eye replied, "please forgive me and accept my apology but because Eye ate a little something prior to leaving the house Eye never offered you anything. Would you like a smoothie? She said sure as she went into her wallet to buy them, but Eye couldn't allow that. Eye purchased both smoothies and she gave me her business card and asked me to call her later that evening. Eye must say that she was very respectful, attentive to the things we conversed about and her smile was as innocent looking as her demeanor. She asked if she could have a hug? Eye said sure and she hugged me as if she was in heaven and never wanted that moment to end.

Eye left the shopping mall and went back to the house feeling thankful for the support that Eye received for my book. Eye was elated that someone long distance felt the passion and received the message portrayed in the book. Later that evening, around 9:00p.m. Eye called Alicia and we continued our conversation from earlier for another two hours. She invited me to meet her at Arizona restaurant for dinner that next evening as she stated, "I'd like to talk business with you." Eye responded, "what kind of business?" She enthusiastically replied, "more people need to read your book. You need to be come a brand, a household name. I can place you in the major markets." "Really", Eye replied. Meet me tomorrow evening, at 5:00p.m. at the restaurant and we can see what direction we'll flow. Needless to say, that Eye was a little reluctant to go but she was talking my language, especially branding "Bishops Need Love Too."

Don't ever deceive YOURSELF!!

YOU have aspirations, goals, ambitions, the power to dream, think and envision.

The moment you STOP is the moment you give your life away.

Your purpose is to make your dreams/visions a REALITY!!

BEWARE though because there are people that you've allowed in your circle that are listening to your ideas you're making public. These people are impostors whom you THOUGHT were your friends or close family members.

(1) Why are they stealing your ideas?
(2) Why have they decided to get closer to your "friends" and make them their very own?
(3) Why are they trying their best to dismember or degrade you behind your back?

ANSWER: Insecure "mutha fukkas" thrive on living in the confines of the lies they create for themselves and accept the lie as their reality. "NOTHING FROM NOTHING LEAVES NOTHING!"

The people that makes the decision to be-LIE-ve them and connect with them are better off with them, TRUST ME!

Iron sharpens iron as flies go hard for a pile of shit!

REMAIN FOCUSED or time will pass you by and you'll begin reflecting on your past only to realize that you've birthed so many millionaires or billionaires; but you're still at the beginning of the circle.

You've been wondering why you've been seeing the same old things, attracting the same type of folk and engaging in the same old conversations without evolving in your travels.

You've been on a solar powered Ferris wheel and didn't know it.

This is YOUR time, YOUR NOW.... MAKE YOUR LIFE WORK for YOU!

When situations occur that relieve you of some folk, ACCEPT IT!! Don't ask questions, don't get upset, don't argue, don't cry, don't worry but be EXTREMELY HAPPY.

The vindictive will easily connect with its kind as with the schizophrenic, the liar or deceiver. The reason it's NOT as easy to connect with you is because your innermost radar can pick up on their bullshit! - Lamont Bershawn

We're now at Arizona's restaurant near the shopping mall that we initially met. She said, "I just wanted to thank you for the uplifting conversations. I didn't think it was possible that anyone could answer most of my religious questions in a book. I don't want you to think that I'm desperate or coming onto you {usually when a person says that, it usually means the opposite} but you're a brilliant and amazing man." "Thank you so much", Eye replied. "So, what type of business proposition did you want to talk about?" {Eye wanted to cut to the chase so that we'd remain focused on what this dinner was really about}.

EYE'VE STOOD INSIDE THE EYE OF HELL AND REMAINED FEARLESS!

Man, she blew me away when she pulled out her portfolio. She was definitely educated and had her business in order {so Eye thought}. She told me about her two daycare centers, the limousine business she was about to enter, joint mortuary business with her Aunt, dessert catering business, etc. She had the graph chart, dates and numbers to match everything she discussed. She pulled out college articles that awarded her six figured awards and said she wanted to take me to a new level. While she was on a roll seeing that Eye was becoming more interested in a business venture with her she pulls out her bank account information which at that time had $82,000.00 in it.

Eye still wasn't the least impressed because in the back of my mind Eye was feeling no one wants to invest in you without receiving a beneficial return. Eye was in awe and had to process the entire conversation. When Eye arrived back at the house Eye began preparing to leave the next morning, heading back to my home. A few hours later Alicia called me and asked if she could drop by for a few minutes. Against my better judgment Eye said, "yes." When she dropped by, she brought four homemade cupcakes and a thank you card with $100.00 in it. Eye had no idea she was fattening me up for the kill. Eye invited her downstairs in the den because Eye was in the process of watching a good movie. Alicia's cupcakes tasted like they were made by a professional baker at a bakery. When Eye finished eating my cupcake Eye alluded to the fact that Eye needed to shower up and get my rest. She apologized for keeping me up and asked if she could get a "see you later" hug. Once again, Eye obliged as she kissed me on the cheek, while her hand gently gripped my manhood as it began to "stand at attention." Alicia knew exactly where she wanted this to go and she knew exactly what to do. She quickly dropped to her knees and began sucking my erect penis until Eye erupted in her mouth, swallowing every ounce of my nectar.

When she stood up she said, "you must drink plenty of pineapple juice because your cum was sweet and not bitter." Eye replied, "Eye take very good care of myself." Eye assumed she was used to sucking dick just by her statement but didn't want to judge her. Again, what was her ultimate goal or motive for the surprising gifts {50-inch flat screen television, brand new 8gb Dell laptop "Amethyst" to signify my birthstone, chemist to make personal fragrance, etc.}. Needless to say, that Eye slept pretty well that night.

When Eye arrived home Alicia texted me to see had Eye made it home safely. Eye let her know that Eye'd made it home and that Eye'd call her once Eye got settled. When Eye got settled Eye honored my word and called her. We talked approximately thirty minutes as she was adamant about making my name a brand, but Eye knew there would be strings attached. Once again, Eye let her know that Eye wasn't interested in a relationship with her and it wasn't necessary to buy me gifts, her word was good enough for me. Alicia's response was a little shocking as she stated, "As long as you'll allow me to swallow your sweet sperm and you can handle it without getting attached I'm all in."

Eye was taken back but replied, "Alicia Eye assure you that Eye'm not going to get attached but Eye don't want a business friendship to go sour in the event Eye begin to desire a relationship outside of this friendship. Eye don't want anyone's feelings to get hurt." Alicia quickly turned back to business saying, "Now that we have an understanding I'm going to contact the chemist in the morning to design two fragrances for you to smell. How's your schedule next Friday?" Eye told her that Eye was free. Friday came and she arrived, rented a car, got to her hotel room and called me to let me know that she was going to shower get dressed and she'd be to my house within a couple of hours to pick me up.

Alicia arrived at my home a couple of hours later and we went to dinner to go over the details concerning the fragrance. She pulled out agreement forms, contracts, percentage sheets, graphic charts and two tubes of a portion of the fragrances she wanted me to smell. She was definitely a business minded woman that night and Eye was amazed that she had every "I" dotted and every "T" crossed. To be totally honest, Eye loved her business sense, her mindset when it came to marketing and promoting but wasn't physically attracted to her at all. The business meeting was over and because it was the weekend she asked me if Eye had any plans. We ended up at the casino for a few hours playing slot machines, winning and really enjoying ourselves.

EYE'VE STOOD INSIDE THE EYE OF HELL AND REMAINED FEARLESS!

It was late and she was tired. She asked if we could go to her room for an hour so she could get a powernap before taking me home. Eye live thirty minutes away and was concerned about her safety and Eye didn't want her to end up in an accident, so Eye went to her room and dozed off in the chair. Eye can't recall how long Eye was asleep but Eye awakened to Alicia "giving me head" while wearing a black teddy with her 44 DD tits hanging out. This time Eye stood up while she was sucking my dick and Eye got butt naked laying her on the bed looking at her shaved, wet pussy and Eye fucked her like there was no tomorrow.

A few hours later she dropped me off home. Eye hopped in the shower thinking, "What the fuck just happened?" Eye called Alicia after Eye got dressed and she sounded like she was on cloud nine and hit the Powerball. "Are you okay?", Eye asked. Alicia responded, "*Yes, I had an amazing time with you. Nobody has ever made me feel that way. It's as if my body was being sculpted like a masterpiece by Picasso. Oh yeah and I just want you to know that having sex with you is one of the most bizarre things I have experienced to date. At first, I didn't get what was going on with my body and it actually took me some days to figure it out. Basically, the experience is like no other when you touch my body I feel a sensation come over me, but when you entered my body I was completely taken by what happened to me. It was the best thing I have ever felt.*" "Yes, Eye had a great time as well Alicia but Eye don't want it to destroy our business intention", Eye replied. "Now don't get foolish, we already agreed that our interest isn't involving ourselves in a relationship", Alicia responded. Eye felt relieved for a moment after hearing those words come from her mouth.

This is my last night up here and Eye'd like to take you and your mother to dinner, is that okay? Sure Alicia, we'll meet you at 8:00 p.m. at Golden Corral. "Perfect", responded Alicia. We had an enjoyable evening conversing and eating. Alicia didn't want the evening to end that early so she suggested we go to the casino for an hour. Upon our arrival, Alicia handed my mother a card with $500.00 in it. My mother asked, "What's this for?" "For giving birth to a magnificent and brilliant man, your son Lamont the genius", Alicia responded.

Mom said, "thank you but you didn't have to give me anything." It was at that moment Eye knew Alicia was trying her best to develop a close friendship with my mother in order to get closer to me. Alicia then handed me five one hundred-dollar bills and said, "let's go hit a jackpot or have some fun." No one hit the jackpot but we had fun playing the slots.

When my mother and Eye left the casino, my mother looked at me and said, "Alicia seems like a nice young lady but be careful because she has a hidden motive and agenda to get closer to you." In other words, my mother was confirming that which Eye already felt.

Things were quiet for a few weeks as Alicia and Eye probably spoke twice in a three-week period. Alicia called me one afternoon and started crying on the phone. Eye asked her, "Why are you crying?" Alicia responded, "I'm tired of doing so much for people and all they do is give me their ass to kiss." Eye quickly interjected as if Alicia was referring to me, "This is why Eye asked you not to go out of your way with these surprising gifts. Eye don't ever want you to think that Eye'm one to take advantage of you." Alicia replied, "I'm not talking about you Lamont." Alicia proceeded to say, "My mother doesn't appreciate a fucking thing I do for her. I'm paying for her monthly mortgage, furnished her home, give her a monthly allotment and all of that after she abandoned me as a child and allowed her husband to molest me. Where was her God in my moment of turmoil? I went on to finish college without her help and made something of myself through all of the pain, hurt and misguidance. Yet, she tells me to pray to a mother fucker that never seems to answer anyone's prayers."

Eye felt saddened by the story she'd given me and was speechless for a moment. Eye didn't know whether Eye should hang up the phone and allow Alicia to vent or continue to be a listening ear. It was then Eye knew she was dealing with extensions of hurt and hadn't received any form of relief. Eye thought to myself, "How can a Clinical Psychologist {that's what she told me her main occupation was} help people or allow them to identify with their internal issues and she hadn't really dealt with her very own?"

Alicia began to really open up to me about her marriages, children, her businesses that weren't doing so well and how she coped with handling all of it. Eye asked her how did her ex-husband deal with the mental aspect of you once being molested? Alicia said, "Her husband didn't eat pussy so he had someone else eat her pussy and when it was time for the penetration he'd send ask them to leave and then he'd step in." Once again, Eye'm on the phone speechless. Eye asked her how did that make her feel? Alicia responded, "It no longer mattered to me just as long as I was being satisfied. My feelings for my husband was diminishing and we were on the verge of divorcing anyway."

If you're in an abusive {psychologically, emotionally, financially, physically, etc.} marriage. GET THE FUCK OUT NOW {GTFON}!!

Eye know that some of you take pride in living according to your religious beliefs, values and view. Deep down in your spirit you want to leave but you're waiting on a sign, word or message from "God" because the abuse that you're experiencing just isn't good enough for you to leave.

Eye'm sure that some of you ladies have taken your vows serious in hopes that your spouse will remain on one accord with you. The preacher allowed you to believe that you're to remain married until a physical death, regardless of any situation.

Please understand this and Eye hope it gives you the strength to awaken to your reality. You're not required to stay in any abusive situation. Eye know you probably attend church daily and are a regular at the altar and either the "Mother of the church" {usually an older missionary that's a widow} or some other brainwashed or hurt woman is telling you:

(1) Remain strong because God's going to use you to save your husband and this will be your testimony.
(2) Don't run from that which God ordained.
(3) This is only a TEST.
(4) Keep the faith. What God has joined together, let not man put asunder.

Everyone's marriage is different; therefore, the best advice is the advice coming directly within your own heart/ feelings; however, most of you women miss it because you're believing that God is speaking to you through what is defined as religious scripture.

Are you experiencing a psychological breakdown in your marriage? This is a disorder that manifests primarily as severe stress-induced depression, anxiety or dissociation in a previously functional individual. The individual is no longer able to function on a daily basis. This is also known as a nervous breakdown.

Are you an emotional wreck due to the infidelity that has taken its place in your marriage? You find it hard to trust any man because of what you've experienced with the men you've been involved with. Well, all men aren't the same therefore choose wisely.

Often times a person will experience a "Spiritual death/ Spiritual Disconnection" and a "Physical Dismembering" prior to the "Physical death."

The spiritual death is totally connected to your spirit, which are inner feelings/ emotions. These feelings are TRUE and are NOT to be discounted, overlooked or set aside.

EYE'VE STOOD INSIDE THE EYE OF HELL AND REMAINED FEARLESS!

Here's a few examples of a "Spiritual death": (1) When you're feeling lonely/ alone in the presence of your spouse. Isolation (2) When you no longer can stand being intimate with your spouse (3) When you become numb to anything your spouse says (4) When you find yourself taking long hours to even come home to be in the company of your spouse, etc.

If you've gotten to the point in your marriage that you're no longer living/ loving and maintaining a healthy attitude then it's imperative to make a few changes. You've become physically drained, spiritually impaired and religiously indoctrinated to the point that you don't know which way to turn.

Always remain true to yourself, your feelings and your nature. In a marriage, you still MUST maintain your individuality and fulfill the necessary desires or a partnership. "Two people from different backgrounds and experiences trying to build an empire!!"

If you've done everything respectful to please your spouse, yet they refuse to appreciate you. STOP!!

Your light is currently dim because of your situation and you're experiencing darkness because there's a disconnection but still plenty of wattage within you. Connect with someone that will illuminate your power, not someone that constantly disregards it!! – Lamont Bershawn

Eye began to ask Alicia was that the reason she became an Atheist? Alicia responded, "My mother's whorish lifestyle and the period I was being molested I had nobody to protect me. I was taught to pray, fast and call on the name of Jesus/ God and they would show up. Well, no one heard me scream, no one heard me cry and no one believed me not even my mother." Alicia was carrying so much pain and this pain was still in a deep place stemming from her childhood and more in her adult life.

Alicia and Eye stopped communicating for a couple of months. While on Facebook Eye received a message from Alicia's ex-husband. He sent me a message saying, *"Hey man my wife well ex for now told me that I could find you on facebook.. I just wanted to stop by and let you know man your book was on point. Alicia presentation of your book had all my co-workers begging for more and buying your book you picked the right person she can sell a dead man a coffin. I like the way yall hooked up the entire scenario with the life size poster, food, and the prizes yall gave away damn man that's what up. Imma tell like this my ex wife is a handful, but she know how to make shit happen though. All the fellas down here in my squad reading your book man...she sold them books like crack cocaine lmao glad I got it man good luck and I cannot wait for your next one. Man, I grew up in the Catholic church and I always knew it was a bunch of shit going on that they covered up. Thanks man I wish you well I know fe fe will let me know about the next book. Peace!*

> *June 20th, 1:48am*
>
> *Hey man I hope it's ku with u that i follow your post. I hit u up earlier in the inbox to tell you who I was and how much I enjoyed your book. Keep doin wat you doin man.*
>
> *Look here man you ain't gotta say nuthing back and I knoe yo u want cuz u never answerd my other messages. I don't know you, but I read your book and your post and I respect what you stand 4 man I was never able to feel free about my religious teachn like I do now. I just want to know and u can call me if u prefer why you neva around when my ex wife promoting*

EYE'VE STOOD INSIDE THE EYE OF HELL AND REMAINED FEARLESS!

yo books sales? Again, I helpd her today set up another book fair sellin ur shit and u not there to greet the people. I asked her she just said she didnt know wtf is that all about? Look, it is not my business wat you do or how u do man I respect you man to man, but she workn her ass of selling your stuff and don't know why u not there. She says u know nuthin about it, but she was stuck with all the stuff she bought or whatevea. I ain't making no waves or problems, but I know this woman well she don't put time and energy into somethin unless she has good reason. Man she sold dozens of ur books, tshirts, and other stuff today like crack cocaine. She run out books she started ordering people books online. Now i helped her set up and clean up where was u? Again not making a problem just concerned, becuz her health man she is not physically in the right shape for all this. Last nite she was sick, but she stayed up all night cooking shit for this damn book fair and u the star and not there. Of course outta concern cuz I love that woman we not together no more, but i hope one day we will. I want to know why she doin it for u she won't say nuthin. She handmade 50 glasses last night until 2 in the morning for yo shit wit yo name on it. I just think either u don't know she doin or you an ungrateful person, so I just thought I asked u she ain't sayin nuthin. She made all that money and said it was goin in a fund for your business start up wtf. She did not take a single dime either she believes in u or luv u man..whatever it is u dead wrong for not thankn her I watched her work hard. She done this 2 weeks in row to make ur shit sell neither time ur were there.

She don't know I talked 2 u, becuz she is going thru enough right now, but if u tell her its cool 2 I just not tryn to worry her she real sick these days. Yo man here is my number if you wanna call me cool if not i ain't trippin. Keep doin what you doin man I love ur book!"

Eye immediately responded, "Hello my brother. Eye didn't know of any book signing that was supposed to benefit me or on my behalf. Eye would never disappoint people taking the time to support my book. Who gave the book signing and where was the venues location?" He replied, "My ex-wife Alicia. It was at a banquet hall in Georgia." Eye immediately ended the conversation and contacted Alicia. When Eye contacted Alicia Eye asked her, "When did you have a book signing for me and who authorized you to do so?" Alicia said, "I had a book signing on your behalf but I didn't tell you because I was a little upset with you because in the midst of me breaking down you didn't catch a plane here to console me." Eye flipped, "Are you out of your fucking mind? This is why Eye never mix business with pleasure. How much money did you make off of the event? Where's my percentage? As a matter of fact, I'm going to need everything used for the event." Alicia booked a flight for that weekend and rented a car. When she arrived to my home she had three dimensional creations she made, different original posts by me on every table, fragrance marketing posters, and little favors with the book title on it. She bought me a few articles of clothing with some of the money from the event {shirts, pants, vests, shoes, etc.}. Eye simply told her never to do that again and she agreed not to.

Eye'm guessing that Alicia felt some sort of way that her ex- husband contacted me as well as one of her girlfriends. Alicia thought that her girlfriend, Cindy liked me and thought the feelings were mutual. Cindy just wanted to let me know that Alicia held an event that Eye was a no show which made me look bad. Cindy knew exactly how cunning Alicia was and wanted to alert me to what was going on because Cindy didn't believe that Eye was the type of person that would ignore my very own book signing, Eye wasn't. When Alicia found out that Cindy contacted me Alicia began slandering Cindy's name with allegations that she was HIV positive, a whore and that she took care of her to prevent her from being homeless. Eye clearly told Alicia that Eye'm not interested in either of you and Eye find it highly offensive for you to tell Cindy's personal business, if it's true.

> *"If a person will tell a lie for you, they'll damn sure lie to you so don't sleep because that same person will tell a lie on you!!"* – Lamont Bershawn

Alicia began to show me her bitter and conniving side and Eye explained to her that it was best that we part ways because Eye was no longer comfortable with the way she was doing things. Alicia was a bitter, scorned and bipolar woman who was not only a danger to society but also to herself. Eye asked Alicia, "Have you ever tried to commit suicide?" Alicia didn't hesitate to answer with a profound YES. Eye didn't want her to go into detail about it, Eye just was wondering because it seemed as if she was fighting a battle from within her own mind. Alicia and Eye stopped talking. Eye blocked her from calling, texting and emailing me. Two months later she flew into town and Eye received a call from an unknown number at 2:00a.m. It was Alicia crying and apologizing to me for the things she said in the prior months. She asked if we could meet up at the casino tomorrow afternoon. Eye agreed.

We met the next afternoon and we decided to grab a bite to eat. She still wanted to make "Bishops Need Love Too" a brand and continue with the fragrance. Alicia began holding her head down and Eye asked if something was wrong? Alicia said, "I need to be honest with you but I'm afraid that you'll never talk with me or trust me again." Eye said, "What is it?" Alicia replied, "When we weren't speaking I took it upon myself to contact Jerome, your younger brother because I wanted to be vindictive. We talked on the phone for two weeks but I realized that his conversation wasn't on the same level as yours. I drove six hours to meet him at his house and we drove another six hours to Cherokee, NC to the Indian reservation. We stayed a few hours and then I dropped him off, changed clothes and drove back home. I did it to hurt you or get back at you for not speaking with me." Eye wasn't hurt in the least but Eye felt betrayed because Jerome knew of her cunning ways through their conversation, yet he still indulged in her foolishness. Alicia read and understood what Eye wrote in my book concerning my family, yet she took it upon herself to dishonor our friendship.

Eye told Alicia, "You did your best to try and hurt my feelings but it all backfired on you. Eye bet you feel used because he probably told you that you're not his type and he took advantage of you because he saw a thirsty, gullible and vulnerable little girl. You're used to "buying" people's love, affection and attention because your self-esteem is very low. Eye can't be purchased. Eye can no longer trust you and now you're dead to me, goodbye!"

A few weeks later Eye received this letter from Alicia in my email: {Actual email}

"Hello Lamont,

I am finally resting my brain here in AC right now and I feel a sense of peace I brought my daughter with me after yesterday incident did not want to leave her at home. Anywho I wanted you to know that I cherish our friendship greatly and that I never want to come off to you as some drama filled person who life is out of control. Well actually to be honest that is what it looks like right now. Allow me to explain what is going on briefly as I can. As I told you around July of this year I was set up by my best friend for a check scam, and she also invaded my emails, and she took my private journal and shared things with men in my life past and present. I got over it moved on and kept it moving. Well it seems as if the after effects of that journal was still causing others

EYE'VE STOOD INSIDE THE EYE OF HELL AND REMAINED FEARLESS!

to have ill will towards me. During this same time frame I was robbed at gunpoint at the ATM machine after leaving my daycare these guys were caught and has been charged with strong arm robbery the DA kept the case as you know I was in pretrial hearings all last week. Anyways, I could not prove she had anything to do with that and I cannot blame anyone for that but myself. So again, I brush shit off and decide to go get my open carry gun permit and learn how to properly handle a weapon and I did what I needed to do to feel safe. Again, I move on not creating any drama or bothering anyone. Apparently, the Investigators felt they did not have enough evidence to charge them with fraud stealing my check, so they dropped the charges. Again, I am cool just moving on as usual. Now the situation arise with the facebook situation and Rodney whoever else and him or whoever contacting you. By no means did have anything to do with that my only part I played in the situation was telling you he was an alright person and you took my word and added him. Whoever and he is not clean in the situation took part in contacting you I confronted the situation as a grown person to seek closure and let him and whoever else know look I am not with this type of madness it makes no sense to act like high school kids let it go. I think it is all over things are done I said what I needed to say as a grown up and again I had moved on. Well, on Tuesday of this week I get a call from a professional not a casual associate they alert me to go check my website out ASAP it was something bad on there. I go check my website out and in the comment section at the bottom again I cannot blame anyone without proof, but some things you just know…it is 10 photos of me and my ex-husband in sexual positions and nude. I called the guy who does my IT work and he could not remove the comments so he ended up having to kill my entire web page altogether. Rodney is a low down dog he was the only one who had access to those pictures the only one who knows my webpage address outside of business people, but he denied having anything to do with it. The next day, he comes up to my office and tells me he didn't do it but being that I am allowing another man to drive the car that is in his name he demands I turn the vehicle over to him or he will take me to court and sue me for the car. I told him to get the fuck out my office and life to kiss my ass it is my car I paid for and paid him to register the vehicle for me. So, this week I went to the Tag Office and removed his name off the vehicle, but my car now has no tags on it. I took the vehicle to my new condo and placed it in the garage, because it is tagless. No one I mean no one except contractors and furniture delivery people have my new address I refuse to put anything in my name using that address everything will come from the old address still. Anyways, fast forward to Thursday of this week this bastard has the nerves to tell me that he is going to sue me, because he is entitled to half of what I made during our marriage although we were separated at the time. So whatever bitch he is dealing with she seems to think she is smart and putting shit in his head for whatever reason.

EYE'VE STOOD INSIDE THE EYE OF HELL AND REMAINED FEARLESS!

Point is he read my journal, because in my journal I made a few statements about buying you a car or letting you use the other car and he ran away with that although it never actually happened. So, he seems to feel slighted and much of his feelings excuse me for being explicit stems from him reading how I enjoyed sucking your dick and tasting your cum, because all the years we were together I never did that with him. He did have something to do with those messages he might not have been the one typing it, but he was dictating it. Now, the reason I am emailing you this and not telling you on the phone 1. I know you are out of town and so am I. 2. I do not discuss things like this in front of my baby girl. Now, Saturday morning mind you the Avenger is not at the house and so happen I take my Kia to the dealer on Friday so they can fix on it while I am gone. I did not worry about it because I was using my cousin's car no big deal right? Apparently, it appeared as if I was not at home to a would be robber. Me and my daughter was actually sitting at the table eating some oatmeal and we kept hearing this pecking sound we actually thought it was a squirrel or woodpecker chewing on the house. A few minutes later we hear the sound of broken glass I am like what the fuck, before I could get up the alarm went off. I tell me daughter to call the police and I go in my room retrieve my weapon and scour through the house I see a back window was cracked. I go to the front door and look out the glass pane inside the door I see this fool running from house he came from the side of it. I did not see his face, but we did get a description of his clothing and build.

My daughter who was on the phone with the police gives them a description of what we saw. WIthin 5 minutes an officer was at our home they checked the perimeter and the interior and found no one. They found a screwdriver on the ground near that rear window and the screen was on the ground also. He was actually trying to pry the window out, but he cracked the window in the process which made the alarm go off. Seems bizarre and far fetched which is why tok pictures of this fool no one would believe this bullshit otherwise. I also got the police report if you want to see that as well. I took a step back from you, because of all of this bullshit I am currently dealing with. I do not want anything coming your way and this is my mess that I need to fix. I have never dealt with some much at once, but it is only making me stronger Lamont. I can tell you this much I promise you when this all calms down I will be super cautious about the things I do, I say, and the people I deal with. I know you are not going to read all of this, but I do want you to know that I respect our friendship and will not bring anything negative your way." -Alicia.

Eye read the letter, but this time Eye knew who Eye was dealing with. To cross the line with a family member is the line that will end a friendship. People fail to realize there's a spiritual bond between brothers that's impossible to break for the simple fact they come from the same womb. Physically, psychologically, financially they may differ but having a common denominator as a mother is priceless.

Yesterday was the first time in six months since my brother and Eye have spoken. He flew out to Atlanta to support the event. We shook

EYE'VE STOOD INSIDE THE EYE OF HELL AND REMAINED FEARLESS!

hands hug one another and told each other that we loved each other, that was a priceless moment.

Eye heard someone say, "look at what prayer can do." Eye kindly responded, "this wasn't prayer. We just decided to place our differences aside and respect each other."

Life's too short for the bullshit. Especially, to allow other people's mess to infiltrate FAMILY OR a brotherhood.

ALWAYS BROS. BEFORE HOES!!! - Lamont Bershawn.

Jerome knew exactly what he encountered when he met Alicia. Jerome decided to take it upon himself to introduce Alicia to Kurt, who was still incarcerated. Kurt was our oldest brother who was framed for murder and was doing a double life bid for his conviction. Alicia sent her information to Kurt so the prison society could approve her for future visitation. Alicia still had a motive for trying her best to get my attention. Alicia knew that when Eye decide to dismember, disassociate and disconnect from anything or anyone it wasn't hard. Kurt called me one day and asked me, "How do you feel about Alicia?" Eye responded, "Eye don't feel anything for her. She's not to be trusted. Alicia's vindictive, bipolar, cunning and the only reason she's visiting you is to learn all she can about your situation. Be careful of what you discuss with her because when things don't go her way, she's going to betray you." Kurt fell victim into Alicia's web and married her.

Kurt's dad, Harry aided in making Kurt marry Alicia. It was a business proposition because Alicia is financially stable and could take over assuming the legal bills as Kurt's wife. Alicia didn't understand that she was making a deal with another devil, Harry because he was divorcing his wife, Janice after forty-nine years and he knew he'd legally be forced into giving Janice half of what was accrued during the marriage.

All of this wasn't anything new to Harry, although he and Janice had been married forty-nine years. Seven years into the marriage Harry and one of his mistresses had a little girl. Janice still honored her marriage, her husband and her family through fasting and praying. Eye'm not saying Janice wasn't hurt, but she carried it very well without getting out of character. Eye mean not in front of her children anyway.

Alicia still tried her best to connect with me through social media. She'd continue following my posts without commenting until she found out that Eye was about to get married to Candace. Candace had many followers and was used to posting all of her personal business. Alicia wouldn't ever comment on my page because she was blocked. Somehow, she'd comment on Candace's page slandering my name. Eye suppose she'll never get over being rejected by me after all she should be happy after marrying someone who was convicted of murder and may never see freedom again. Alicia's conscience was eating herself up because everything she tried to do to get my attention wasn't penetrating me at all. Candace could pretty much see that Alicia was a scorned woman who just refused to get the picture. Eye was totally honest with Candace concerning Alicia and backed everything Eye said with emails. Candace felt relieved to know Eye wasn't telling her a lie. Eye told Candace Eye'd never lie to her because lying wouldn't give her the right to make a decision based from the truth.

Alicia made one final attempt to contact me, labeling it "One Last Cry." {Actual email}

"Hello Lamont,

> *I am not perfect, I have made mistakes, I have said the wrong things, done the wrongs, made bad choices, had to live with poor decisions, but I am by no means a bad person. I had to face my own realities this past week as I took a week vacation and spent time with myself in Atlantic City. I learned that I am not perfect*

that I am perfectly imperfect. I was always viewed as being the strong person in my family I was never able to show any weakness, because everyone always relied on my strength to carry the family through crisis. I most certainly had to face my own issues and my pain that I carried around for many years and passed on into relationships and friendships. I realized that I did carry a whole lot of pain and hurt inside of me, and it has probably been the poison that has killed many of my friendships. What I have also learned is that everyone that enters your life has some sort of value to contribute to it even if it is for a short time. I just wanted to take this time to let you know that I really do appreciate all the valuable deposits that you made into my life, and as I did a lot of self-reflecting all of the positive things that you passed on to me become transparent and applicable to my life.

I grew up in a single- family home my mother had 2 children my sister and I. I was the black sheep and my mother never loved or paid attention to me like she did my sister. I was always in the shadows of my mother's thoughts. She took care of me and kept me fed, but she never showed one iota of interest in me or any type of love towards me. My sister was her love child the one that she laughed with, took the time, shared special moments with, and she adored her over me. I never knew who my father was, because my mother would never tell me. For many years I longed to have a father figure in my life, but never got one. I have come to terms that none of that was my fault nor will any of it define me as a person now. Much of my pain stemmed from my childhood as I was physically abused and molested by one of my mother's husbands for many years. Inadvertently, It caused me to look at men in a negative light, because the only impression that I had of a man in my life was negative. I essentially thought all men were out to hurt me and meant me no good based on my experience of a "father" in my life. I had actually molded myself to think that a man was always going to do something to me negative, and I was wrong. I never actually faced this pain, but I concealed this pain for many years trying not to show any weakness. I thought I had put a lot of this pass me, but I didn't never really get a chance to cry and let out all the emotions from this pain. Don't get me wrong I have cried over it, but I have never cried for myself and the mental pain. Well, I finally had one last cry it was not a sad cry nor was it a happy cry, but it was a cry of freedom from the mental grips that it had on my life. I was hurting really bad and did not know it on the surface. I felt that my mother sold me out for a man and that she never liked or loved me anyways, but now I am her favorite go figure. I was finally able to face what I had suppressed for over 30 years. I always was able to cover up my pain, but again every person you meet is bringing something valuable to your life like it or not. If it wasn't for me meeting you and falling in love with you I would have never been forced to face it, and now the healing will begin for me. I appreciate you for passing through my life. I respect and understand your decision to detach yourself away from me, because no one needs a weak link in their life that has been hurt deeply. I had never in my entire life experienced love until I met you Lamont, but I honestly did not know how to deal with that love or understand it. Being that I can from a severely dysfunctional background love is not something that I ever dealt with, so when it came it was like foreign to me. I didn't mean to spoil our friendship with it, but it was like I had entered into the twilight zone and I really had no experience with love. I will admit I did and said some dumb stuff, because again I was afraid and feared feeling LOVE it was totally foreign to me. I have never been spiritually connected to anyone in my entire life NEVER. I did not know how to handle it which is obvious being that I screwed it up. However, I do appreciate you for everything.

I am not going to say that I am sorry for disrespecting your wishes to never contact you again, because I am not sorry. I really needed to thank you and let you know that I appreciate our season we had. I felt like sharing what I went through with you, because I have no one else that in this entire world that I feel comfortable enough to share "me" with, and not be judged or ridiculed. Again, it was me just wanting to share and thank you for all that you have given me internally to help me spiritually regain self.

I know you will be blocking this email also and I am fine with that you should dislike me for all the rotten things I have said, and I did not really mean them. I will just leave with this: I am sorry that I destroyed our friendship it was not my intentions. If you ever feel like forgiving me you know how to reach me, and if you never forgive me that is also fine. I wish you the best in life you know how I feel about your talents and gifts and I wish you nothing but pure success. Also, I will be in Philly for my birthday so if you care to have dinner, cuss me out, ignore me, gamble with me, or just look at me from a distance without saying a word. I will be in your area from August 29th - September 1st and you know where you can find me at. Parx Casino did give me some birthday stuff, so you know that is where I will be. I miss your mother too I really do she is so sweet, and I admire her strength and unconditional love that she has for others. I know I will be blocked indefinitely I know i know i know. - Alicia

THIS IS YOUR CONSCIENCE:

In case you're wondering what/ who Eye am? Eye am the awareness of a moral or ethical aspect to your conduct together with the urge to prefer right over wrong. Eye am the part of the superego in psychoanalysis that judges the ethical nature of your actions and thoughts and then transmits such determinations to your ego for consideration. Eye am the place that house the information from Most High, Supreme Architect, God, etc. that takes PRECEDENCE over any book or resource because Eye am connected to the SOURCE that controls YOU!!

Many of you have questioned me from time to time and ultimately went against me by relying on something you read that didn't even concern you, but you thought that it was needed information. You began to store it within your brain and it became a constant *battle, struggle and fight. Why? It's because you read it and stored the information that totally contradicted the most powerful source that will guide you to success. This is your conscience!!*

Many of you have neglected me because of (1) peer pressure (2) a rough situation (3) negative circumstance (4) "Physically/ Visually Impaired" {you witnessed or actually saw the incident, but misread/ misinterpreted the actual event} (5) "Dedicated Ignorance" {When you know something isn't right but by CHOICE you remain and learn/ embed the material as concrete or absolute} (6) sexual advances {deep down within me, you KNEW you didn't want it but gave it a thought and ended up regretting it - LET'S BE REAL!!}!! This is your conscience!!

Allow me to go DEEPER:

You see the enemy is always on the attack. If the enemy can't get to my "INNER- ME" to devour my "INNER-G", the attack now becomes physical. It causes turmoil wherever it possibly can. This is when Eye {your conscience} steps in letting the enemy know "That no weapon formed against YOU shall prosper."

You see, what the enemy is so confused about is that it tried everything in its power to kill you because it sees what you're bound to become. What the enemy didn't realize was that every time you went to church to hear a sermon, every time you became emotional by listening to gospel music, every time you listened to someone else's testimony {that may have sounded like a similar situation}, every time you prayed {still waiting on an answer}, the enemy didn't get a response. When it threw that very thing that once had you bound and still there was NO REACTION, it didn't recognize that it was no longer living, but now DEAD!! This is your conscience!!

Your flesh gets confused and begins to have a conversation with your spirit!!

Flesh: Why didn't you tell me?

Spirit: If Eye would have told you, we would have never gotten delivered.
Flesh: Eye didn't want to be delivered
Spirit: Eye realized that..lol. That's the reason why Eye was connected to your conscience all along and was preparing for battle.
Conscience: {laughing at flesh} Eye told you never to bring a knife to a gun fight!! Don't you know Eye am the part of the "I AM?" Eye must remain covered and protected at all times. Remember this, while you're resting Eye NEVER Sleep!!

THIS IS YOUR CONSCIENCE!! *– Lamont Bershawn.*

AM EYE MY BROTHER'S KEEPER?

IF YOU HAVE EVER BELONGED to a religious, military, racially deemed supreme, sorority or fraternal organization you've probably been told to ask yourself, "Am Eye my brother's keeper?" This question is given so that you understand the significance of a brotherhood or sisterhood relationship and what it means to be loyal. Most people really don't understand what it means to be loyal because along with loyalty comes respect. It's really impossible or hard for people to give to others what they refuse to give themselves.

In 1997, when Eye joined the Masonic Organization there were two requirements. The first requirement was that Eye had to believe in a "Supreme" being, the second required two Masons had to vouch for my character and bring me in. One of the brother's that brought me in was my biological brother who joined two years prior to me and the other was my play Uncle who at the time was the Past Most Excellent Grand High Priest. Eye should have known there was a weakness in the brotherhood being as though my biological brother was still active and wasn't kicked out because he seemed to always get in some sort of trouble. Eye gave the Masons the benefit of doubt that maybe they could turn his life around for the better.

During the time my group had to show proficiency in front of other brothers to determine whether we could cross over or repeat the class. Eye was the President of my class, so Eye made the commitment to make sure we knew our lines and were sharp using signals and motions. Whenever one of the brothers would stumble Eye was there to make sure they'd remember their part. Eye guess this was the beginning of letting the other brother's see that Eye understood what it meant to have my brother's back. When the question was asked, "Am Eye my brother's keeper?" Eye could strongly answer, "Eye am."

Still being active with the Masonic Organization Eye moved to Florida in 1998. Eye had family member's there and a few friends. My brother Jerome's best friend lived there and he too was a Mason. Actually, he was the President of the line when Jerome crossed over. Ron was a family man and was also in the military. His children called me Uncle and they treated me like family. Ron and Jerome were close and would do anything for each other. Eye mean at least Ron would always do things like invite Jerome to sporting events, birthday parties at their home, special occasions at his wife's job, etc. Eye guess he tried to get Jerome to meet someone special and settle down with a good woman, but Jerome had other things on his mind.

Okay, let's take a step back!

A few years into being a Mason Eye'd go to the cabaret's, the parades and some of the functions or fundraisers at some of the brother's homes. You know Eye just wanted to see who'd show up at times and see what was so special about them. all Eye'll say is they knew how to throw a successful event.

Jerome asked me to ride with him one evening to one of the Masonic events, that's where Eye'd meet Ron and his wife. Ron was a determined brother. Eye mean just his conversation alone was about creating some form of business. He said that his wife had her degree and was a registered nurse, so he knew that he had to get on the ball because he'd soon be discharging from the Navy. Eye could tell that Jerome wasn't paying much attention to Ron because he was trying to talk to every woman that passed by him. We stayed a few hours and then Jerome and Eye left. When we got in the car Eye told Jerome that he should keep Ron as a friend. One thing Eye knew is that good friends pushed their true friends to desire to achieve more and have a better life. Jerome didn't want good friends, he desired those friends that would constantly place him on a pedestal and boost his ego. My guess is he got that from our dad.

EYE'VE STOOD INSIDE THE EYE OF HELL AND REMAINED FEARLESS!

One evening Jerome wrecked his car, but he wasn't hurt. His car only had liability so he was without a car. Eye wasn't one to party or go out many places so Eye'd allow Jerome to drive my car. Jerome and Eye were fairly close until Eye realized that he had no regard for my things and he was just a careless person. When he burned out my clutch to my vehicle and refused to pay a portion of it is when Eye decided to limit his use of my belongings. This would mean that if he had a date either Eye had to take him, he had to catch the bus or find transportation. We'd often double date going to dinner or the movies. It seemed that every time things seemed to be going well something would happen that cause Jerome and Eye to come at odds end. Jerome would have these women that would tell him, "Your brother looks better than you." Eye guess it gave him a complex and that these women would rather date me than him. Oddly enough Jerome began disliking and hating me. Things began getting ugly to the point Eye had to distance myself away from him, so that women he'd begin dating wouldn't even know he had a twin. He'd tell them he had a brother, but not a twin and to make matters worse he'd degrade me so if they ever met me they'd already have a negative mindset about me. Eye had to remember what my mother would always tell me about how Jerome would act as a baby. Eye think this is why Eye'd forgive him so many times because Eye'm the older brother. Throughout our childhood, even up to that point if the question was asked, "Am Eye my brother's keeper?" My answer would have been "Yes."

Ron was going to sea on his last tour before his contract was up. He told Jerome that he'd be relocating to Florida and that he'd keep him posted. Ron asked Jerome to look out for his wife and children while he was away at sea. Meanwhile, the company Eye was working for had an opening in Florida. Two thoughts crossed my mind. First, Eye need to put some distance between Jerome and myself and two, a fresh start. Prior to me heading out to Florida Eye had to briefly stop by my parent's other home to get some of my things. When Eye pulled up to the house the lights were on. This was strange to me because no one was occupying the house at this time, so Eye pulled around back and a black car was parked directly behind the house. As

Eye get out of the car and proceeded to enter the back door, it opens. Walking out the back door was Jerome and Ron's wife. Ron's wife had the look on her face as if she saw a ghost. Eye spoke to the both of them and asked Jerome, "Why are you and Ron's wife over here alone?" Jerome responded, "We had to go over a few things." Eye let that go because Eye knew Jerome was lying.

When Eye arrived to Florida Eye was on a mission. Eye mean Eye was single, didn't have any children, had a good job and was saving money. Eye began networking, working another job, moved into my own place and really didn't have much time to visit family. Eye recall going to the Post Office to send a package to my mother and who did Eye run into? Yep, Ron. Ron looked at me and said, "Eye know this isn't my brother all the way from the City of Brotherly Love! We shook hands and greeted each other with a brotherly hug. We asked how each other's family doing? Then he said, "Tina and the kids are outside in the truck. We're on our way to dinner. Won't you come along?" Eye really didn't want to go because Eye didn't want his wife to get nervous wondering if Eye'd say anything to Ron and also because Eye knew about his wife's infidelity and didn't mention it. Eye was caught between a rock and a hard place.

Eye mean being a twin isn't always as much fun as it's portrayed or people think. People used to always approach us saying, "Eye wish Eye had a twin." Being a twin would be great if both were positive thinking individuals, be great for Hollywood and also great for being a stunt double.

Here Eye am sitting in the presence of my Masonic brother with his family acting as if nothing happened between his wife and Jerome. Is this what a brotherhood consisted of? It wasn't in my eyes. Dinner was great as Eye was able to escape the midst without anyone picking up that my spirit was vexed. Eye went home and couldn't wait to pick up the Bible to see if Eye cold find scripture that would validate Jerome's actions. The closest thing Eye could come up with was Deuteronomy 25:5, "***If brothers are living together and one of them dies without a son, his widow must not marry outside the family. Her husband's brother shall take her and marry her and fulfill the duty of a brother-in-law to her.***" {New International

EYE'VE STOOD INSIDE THE EYE OF HELL AND REMAINED FEARLESS!

Version}. Well, they weren't real brother's and neither of them were dead, so this was considered adultery.

The following weekend Ron asked me to ride with him a few places. We went to the flea market, the PX {Post Exchange} where military people shopped for goods, the auto parts store and grabbed a bite to eat. Ron began asking how Jerome was doing, but Eye did my best to keep every answer pertaining to Jerome extremely short. Ron made the statement, "Eye hope Jerome learned his lesson about chasing pussy." Eye asked Ron, "Why what happened?" Ron said, "Eye had to save his ass on one occasion when a dude caught him in bed with his children's mother. He met this chic at one of our cabaret's that Eye told him not to fuck with because she's flaming. He left with her and before Eye could get out the door they were gone. Eye called him several times leaving messages but Jerome never answered. Eye guess he thought that Eye was "cock blocking." When Eye got hold of Jerome the next day he told me that he fucked her, but he used protection. Now, me knowing Jerome he didn't like using condoms, but maybe he listened to me. Jerome said, "We had sex, she showered and left. Thirty minutes later she called and said that she was HIV positive." Jerome was so scared that he told me that all he could do was go home and hold his daughter in his arms.

Eye was speechless when Ron mentioned these things to me. Now Eye knew there was no way Eye was going to continue a conversation about Jerome. Ron dropped me off and asked me to meet him at his house tomorrow afternoon because Tina was meeting up with her sorority sisters and Eye could potentially meet a friend there. Eye was at their home the next afternoon and we went to the DST {Delta Sigma Theta} function. Eye met a young lady there named Bria. Bria and Eye exchanged information and began dating. This did two things, it kept me from always hanging at Ron's and kept me focused on my relationship with Bria. We had a lot of fun because we enjoyed doing pretty much the same things. Eye helped her with her Spanish class and she was an awesome cook. She was the type of woman that knew how to treat a man. Whenever Eye got off work went home to shower Eye knew dinner would be waiting when Eye arrived. We exchanged keys to each other's place, that's how serious we became. Ron also gave me a key for emergency purposes, but Eye never used it.

Eye never wanted to plant a negative seed in anyone's mind, especially if it could be prevented. Eye've learned that being a "brother's keeper" is extremely hard work, especially if you felt the need to cover or protect one due to their personal and foolish decisions. Jerome always looked at me as the bad guy though and had his constituents believing him, but Eye knew the truth. The difference between he and Eye is that he'll create lies to destroy a person's character but Eye'll tell the truth and present evidence.

> *"One of the MOST DANGEROUS people you'll come across in your life is a habitual liar. They're so hurt to the point they lose their true identity trying their best to be someone they're incapable of being.*
>
> *Most of them are bipolar. They're so envious of you that they begin creating shit in their own minds just to think on your level.*
>
> *The sad part of it is they begin believing their own lies and get viciously upset when people don't go along with them. Real men take care of and claim ALL of their children, their responsibilities and try to live a productive life!" - Lamont Bershawn.*

It never really dawned on me that people would consider twins alike or similar in every way possible. Eye mean we're still individuals and have different minds. Eye'm assuming that people think this way because twins usually are much closer to each other and usually dress alike. We don't share a brain nor do we like the same types of things.

> *"This is going to HELP somebody:*
> *Just because things look alike or similar don't mean they have the same qualities.*

EYE'VE STOOD INSIDE THE EYE OF HELL AND REMAINED FEARLESS!

A Chrysler 300 only look like a Bentley from a distance, but once they're side by side they look NOTHING alike.

Most people won't qualify for the Bentley so they'll settle for the Chrysler 300.

POINT: NEVER settle for LESS than what's desired. You're setting yourself up for a lifetime of misery!!" - Lamont Bershawn.

Here Eye am in Florida living on my own, happy and free from all of the drama and mess especially involving Jerome. Things between Bria and Eye just fell off, but we remained good friends. Eye knew in a couple of months our family reunion would take place here in Florida so Eye was preparing to see relatives that Eye hadn't seen in quite awhile. A few weeks prior Eye had to drive back up north to gather a few things. When Eye arrived Jerome was out of town and come to find out that one of my exes was at my parent's house. She was fresh out of the military {so you'd think she'd either have a place to stay or a few dollars saved up}. This young lady was very attractive but she was scorned deep down within. Eye asked my mother, "Why is she staying here? Don't her mother still live in town?" My mother is a very giving person and opens her heart to the world. Well, come to find out Donna {my ex} mother was evicted from her home and had to move with her brother. Eye knew Donna was still very much in love with me, but in my eyes, she was definitely my past.

When Eye was heading back to Florida she asked if she could tag along just to keep me company for the thirteen-hour ride. Eye allowed her to ride with me, after Eye had an extensive conversation with my mother. When we arrived at my place in Florida, we unpacked the car Eye showed her to her room and we settled in. The next morning Eye had to leave for work and she had breakfast on the stove. She stayed up all night reorganizing my cabinets as if she was going to be there for a minute. Eye made her feel welcomed, took her out to Jazz night, movies and shopping. Eye finally asked her, "You mean to tell me there isn't anyone special in your life?" She responded, "Yes, he's a Mason like you, but you know you'll always be my first true love." As we were having a conversation about him, he calls her phone. She was reluctant on answering the call, but Eye assured her that she could answer the call there's nothing going on between us. The guy she was dating was still in the military but he had no real idea where Donna was. Here Eye am once again thinking, "Am Eye my brother's keeper?" Eye told Donna that she had my blessings in marrying or proceeding with another man because in my eyes as well as my heart the flames went out way before graduating high school. A few days later Eye dropped Donna off at the bus station and she departed with tears in her eyes. A few months later Donna was married. Man, this was a relief Eye thought as if she'd live a happy life with her husband.

Everything was going well and approximately one year later, mom called me telling me that Donna and her husband wanted to know if it was okay to stay with them until they found a place to live? Of course, mom said it was okay. Who brings their husband to stay with their ex-boyfriend parents? Now it was my mother's turn to be the "keeper." Eye assume that Donna never told her husband who this nice lady was because she began calling Jerome her brother, my eldest brother Kurt her brother and Eye was Uncle to her newborn. Yes, she had a child to presumably fill the void she felt from an abandoned relationship with her mother and never knowing her father. Donna and Eye were still pretty much okay with each other and Eye was glad she was married, although Eye knew she didn't marry this guy for love but stability. Donna and Eye had conversations about overcoming her hurt. She began to despise her mother, cuss out her sister because every time she turned around her sister kept having babies that she couldn't support. Donna was really on edge and Eye thought she was going to have a nervous breakdown, a heart attack or commit suicide. It got to the point that we'd talk regularly. She was very active in her church as a "greeter" and participated in other auxiliaries in the church.

Well, Donna always liked the attention of others because she grew up not getting much attention at all. Donna was pretty much the neglected one and her mother would call her, "Cow." Eye thought to myself, "What a fucking insult." Eye thought Donna and Eye were

EYE'VE STOOD INSIDE THE EYE OF HELL AND REMAINED FEARLESS!

pretty cordial until word got back to me that Donna started speaking about my family in such a negative way. Eye had to ask myself, "Is this the same young lady that my Grandmother had to explain how to get a bath as an adult?" "Is this the same young lady that always wanted to spend time at my home?" "Is this the same young lady that wanted to marry me because she was in love with me?" "Is this the same young lady that waited until she was twenty-two to give me her virginity?" "Is this the same young lady that Eye took out of town, bought expensive jewelry for and gave a surprise party for inviting all of her friends?" Eye was taken back for a moment, then Eye realized it is the same woman that desired to be with me but became scorned when she wasn't my choice. Eye guess she had the right to be mad or upset with me because she never had a man that would treat her as well as Eye did. Linda Creed said it best, "The greatest love of all is the love that Eye have for myself."

Jerome heard that Donna was upset and had something against me, so he decided to get in contact with her in order to play on her intelligence. It was just another person that he could get on his team that despised me. Eye began to ask the question, "Why is it so hard for a person to leave well enough alone and create a productive life for themselves, instead of trying to degrade another?" Eye had to dissect this question in order for me to make sense of it. You see it's easy for me to cut, dismember or disconnect myself from anyone that's not beneficial for where Eye'm headed.

LISTEN UP:

People are going to talk about you, degrade you, dislike you, lie on you, steal from you but MOST of all fear YOU; yet they still want to remain attached to you.

"Mutha Fukkas" that constantly want to talk shit about you really desire to be like you but are intimidated by everything you stand for. These are the same "b.i.t.c.h n.i.g.g.a.s"

that build themselves up with lies in order to place themselves on a makeshift pedestal.

Notice there's a (.) after each letter which let you know there's a deeper meaning to the word given. A "b.i.t.c.h" is nothing more than a Broke{n} or Bitter Individual Trying to Cause Havoc and "n.i.g.g.a.s" are Negative Ignorant Guy or Girl After Something.

Be watchful because they'll have you be-LIE-ving their bullshit when in fact the ONLY thing they have going for themselves is gossiping, deceiving, lying, and perpetrating. They're nothing more than leeches trying to suck every ounce of opportunity from you.

Kings and Queens don't allow yourselves to get sidetracked or lose focus. Just KNOW that YOU'RE the ones that are on the correct path. The ones that are talking the MOST shit are the ones that NEED to reevaluate their lives because they're compass has malfunctioned.

"Always keep in mind, a peasant will do whatever it will take to conquer anyone's throne!" - Lamont Bershawn.

Even though Jerome despised me and was building a team full of haters, Eye still loved him because he was my brother. Eye didn't trust him as much but Eye'd give him the benefit of doubt for my mother's sake. Jerome began dealing with a new young lady and he seemed to be head over heels for her. The first thing that came to my mind was maybe she'd make him change his ways for the better. Come to find out, this chic was Jerome's best friend girlfriend and she's more vindictive than he is. This was a code breaker, especially dealing with your best friend's lady. This meant there wasn't any loyalty and could end up in a real bad situation. Funny thing is that evening Jerome's best friend called me and said something didn't seem right with his lady actions. Eye didn't want to tell him that she was involved with Jerome, Eye wanted Jerome to be a man and get things straight with his best friend.

"Am Eye my brother's keeper?" "Yes, Eye am." Eye guess by now some of you are asking, "Why?" It's because Jerome seemed to be doing dumb shit without thinking and eye didn't want my brother dead, but he surely wasn't making things easy. If Eye didn't care Eye wouldn't have covered his ass on numerous occasions. It got to the point that Eye felt the need to protect him and he would think that Eye had nothing better to do than follow him. This brought me back to remembering the time my mother asked Jerome and Eye to go to church with her. During the service the visiting preacher stopped her sermon and pointed into the congregation towards Jerome. She said, "Son, there's a bullet with your name on it." She asked both of us to come up for prayer. She looked at me and said, "Eye'm going to anoint your head, your feet and your hands that wherever he goes you won't. You're a preacher and God is going to draw so many to you." She looked at Jerome and said, "The only reason you're alive is because your brother has been around as your protector when somebody desired to kill you." She looked at my mother and said, "God's going to throw Jerome in jail to get his attention, but don't be upset because it's for his own good." Eye was still very much active in the church at this time and knew what my spirit was feeling but Eye couldn't allow Jerome to get in deep trouble because he had a daughter to raise.

> *"When someone is trying their best to "Kick you under the bus", it's only because they don't realize they're already so far under the bus drenched with oil. It's the oil that have blocked their view of things and is beginning to cause them to suffocate. It's because of you having your hand held out to help them that making it hard for them to accept because of their own guilt. Distressed situations call for desperate measures!!"* -

LAMONT BERSHAWN

POINT: Be careful/ mindful of the bridges you PERSONALLY burn; YOU never know when YOU just may have to cross that bridge again! - Lamont Bershawn.

Eye began feeling like we were in a movie because we weren't raised by our parents to hate or dislike each other. Eye felt like we were in "Money Train", Jerome was Woody Harrelson and Eye was Wesley Snipes. The only difference was they were play brother's and we weren't. In the movie Woody Harrelson always seemed to get himself in trouble because he had a serious gambling addiction and Wesley Snipes would always be there as his protector as well as pull him out of trouble. When a person is addicted to anything it becomes part of who they are and therefore a habit. This was just one thing among many that set Jerome and myself a part. Eye was afraid that one day it would cost some of our mutual and true friends to see us as being the same because we're twins. One of my greatest decisions was to get away as far as possible from Jerome because he was a time bomb waiting to explode and it was only a matter of time. Eye recall receiving a phone call from a mutual friend of ours. He said, "Eye have to apologize to you." Eye responded, "For what?" He began to say, "Just because you're a twin Eye considered the both of you identical in every way, but Eye've come to realize that Jerome is a habitual liar." All Eye could do was feel a sense of relief that someone finally figured it out. Eye accepted his apology and then he began going in detail of some of the lies Jerome told him. To be honest Eye really didn't care about listening, Eye was more pleased with the fact he found out that Jerome and Eye were totally different individuals. It seemed that the more distance Eye placed between the two of us the more people that knew us could see the truth. Then it hit me, "people could never really tell us a part so we both received the blame of doing dumb shit." A few months had gone by and it was around Christmas time.

Eye had to mail off a few things and some Eye had to drop off at United Parcel Service {UPS}. When Eye pulled up to the UPS store, Eye began filling out the information on the cards and boxes.

EYE'VE STOOD INSIDE THE EYE OF HELL AND REMAINED FEARLESS!

On this particular day the weather was pretty nice. As Eye'm sitting in the car Eye could see a young lady to the left of the car just staring at me. When Eye looked up she was looking directly at me so Eye paused from writing. Eye lowered my window to see if she was okay. In essence Eye really wanted to know what she was staring so hard for. She approached the car and asked, "Are you from Philadelphia?" Well, being as though Eye was from Philadelphia but sitting in a parking lot in Georgia sparked my interest. Eye said, "Yes, do you know me from somewhere?" She asked, "Do you have a daughter?" Eye said, "No, but my brother has a daughter." She began describing my house as if she definitely been there before. Eye said, "You thought Eye was Jerome." She responded, "When you began to speak Eye realized that you weren't Jerome because he's an arrogant, conniving, effeminate, punk ass liar." All Eye could do was say, "wow." Eye had to ask her, "What did he do to you?" It seemed as if she had a shopping list of things to say but she just said, "he depicts himself of way more than what he really is." Eye smiled and said, "Yep, that's Jerome." She began tot also say, "Eye never met you because Jerome never wanted me to meet you. Eye guess not because for one you look much better than he does {although you guys are twins} and he destroys your character to make people prejudge you prior to them actually meeting you." My heart was saddened to the fact that Jerome would speak so negatively of me but glad that another person realized who he really was. Eye realized that Jerome {being my brother} was more deadly and dangerous than Eye thought.

> *"When a person will do just about anything {lie, fabricate, mislead} to assassinate a person's character based on their reality it just means it's hard for that individual to accept self. They must now create an alias in which would redirect them from looking at the Medusa of self." - Lamont Bershawn.*

It has always been in my heart to allow people to see or view an individual from their own perception instead of planting any seeds.

The way Eye perceive someone or connect with them may not be the way another person views them, so it's best to just let them judge a person's character by their personal experience.

Eye had my own place in Florida and Jerome wanted to come visit. Eye was reluctant at first but after talking it over with my mother Eye allowed him to come stay with me for a week. The first few days went well probably because Eye was working nights and would drop Jerome off at my grandparents {Eye just didn't trust him being in my home all alone}. Eye knew Jerome was a jealous and envious individual yet Eye still gave him the benefit that maybe he changed his ways. While he was there he met a young lady and she had a girlfriend that he suggested that Eye meet. We decided to go to dinner at Famous Amos one evening, double dating and he began to open his mouth building himself up as if he was Sean "Puffy" Combs or the Sultan of Brunei. Jerome even lied to these women and told them the song they were listening to on the cd was us. They asked him to sing along with it and boy did he sound bad. Eye'll never forget it because he told them that Eye sang the other part of the song. Eye just smiled and closed my eyes because Eye wasn't going to involve myself or engage in his foolishness. Eye really wasn't hungry but it was an open door to break the ice just to see where Jerome's head was. Well, Eye didn't go along with the lies Jerome was telling these women so he decided to try to make me look crazy in front of them. Eye decided to get up and walk away because Eye didn't want to cause a scene nor did Eye desire to make Jerome look like the ass he really was. Little did Jerome know these women were already on to him and his fabrications. Well, Eye did my best trying to be cordial and fix whatever issues he carried in his heart concerning me. This was the beginning of me breaking the mold of me being my brother's keeper anymore. It seemed that every woman he began dealing with would see who Jerome really was. Even to this day Jerome no longer let women know he has a twin brother. The woman he was madly in love with destroyed him and gave him a complex concerning me. Eye was the brother that always had his back even when they said Eye was the "better looking" twin. Eye'd always come back and say that we're identical. Eye wasn't the one being labeled the conceited one,

EYE'VE STOOD INSIDE THE EYE OF HELL AND REMAINED FEARLESS!

the habitual liar, the homosexual {although only a few people knew Jerome liked going into gay clubs and only a few people saw Jerome kiss a man on his penis}, yes it shocked the hell out of me.

Eye asked Jerome was he gay but he always shunned the question. Eye just knew he did a lot of things that straight men would never think of. Eye mean what man wore Ashley Stewart jeans? This was a woman's store. He followed so closely behind our martial arts instructor to the point he was known as his shadow. When the martial arts instructor was caught hugged up with a man in a vehicle Eye knew it was the end of the road with me going to class. Eye mean the martial arts instructor would always have different women over his house daily during class but Eye found out it was all a front. Eye guess some men want people to think they're straight the reason they seem to always have different women around or seek different women out, but they would rather be cuddled up next to a man. No wonder Jerome and our martial arts instructor was so close and understood each other. Then it dawned on me that Jerome could be a bisexual pedophile. Eye say pedophile because Jerome also was propositioning his daughter's girlfriends who were under the age fourteen.

The time was now for me to clean the slate and protect my reputation from Jerome's bitterness, false accusations and lies. Eye was no longer going to leave well enough alone or be passive waiting for some "Lord" to handle it. Eye was no longer going to stand by and allow his lies to destroy another person. Jerome already got his best friend kicked out of the police academy two weeks prior to graduation, yet Jerome didn't mind using his best friend's badge number to get into the movie theater free. Jerome also lied to get me locked up for fourteen hours. Jerome made a negative statement that could have given someone life in prison and last but not least Jerome blackballed a friend by calling the police acting like he was a detective to get him three years behind bars. Yes, Eye had to distance myself because Eye knew doing this type of stuff would get him a free pass to the cemetery. It was time for me to accept our differences and stop making excuses as if everything about us was identical.

Often times we get so caught up trying to be like another person or be on one accord that we get side swiped into the waves and get swept under the currents.

We all endure in what's known as "Truth." There's {My, Our or Their} truth. My truth is the manifestation of my life which became a reality of what Eye was born with, when Eye poured into me. Your truth is what manifests in your life and Our truth is when we meet on one accord, pouring/ investing into us to make things happen.

It's impossible for something to come out, if it was never placed within to begin with.

We as individuals and collective participants must direct our "Energy" {Inner- "G"} in positive places.

"G" {the All- seeing Eye} or secret order which explains the geometrically maneuvering of greatness!!

The {Inner-"G"} is nothing more than the "God" within you. Look at it like this: Many people talk about faith, but faith only moves with "Energy" - the energy of the mind/ thought.

You still ultimately must have the physical "Energy" to move and the spiritual {Inner-"G"} to make it come to pass!!

What's your {Inner- "G"} directed towards? - Lamont Bershawn.

Wait! Allow me to take a few steps back to elaborate on the two times Eye've been arrested. The first time was Mother's Day weekend, 1998. My mother was in Florida visiting my grandmother. Jerome and Eye decided that we'd drive down to also spend the holiday with

EYE'VE STOOD INSIDE THE EYE OF HELL AND REMAINED FEARLESS!

them. Friday evening Jerome and Eye got into an argument over something trivial, but he took it to a different level. This is when

Eye really figured out that he hated me to the point he wanted me dead or he was really mentally disturbed. Eye was in the den talking on the phone with my mother and she asked, "when are we leaving to head to Florida?" Jerome walks in the room to where Eye was standing and said, "Eye should blow your brains out." He left the room and headed upstairs, meanwhile Eye told my mother that Eye'd call her back. Eye wasn't concerned with Jerome getting a firearm from upstairs because my dad had all of his weapons locked up in a safe place and mine was unloaded in a lock safe in the trunk of my car. What Jerome did while being upstairs surprised me to a degree but then again Eye should have known he was up to no good. Eye was still in the den when Eye saw a beam of light flash across the backdoor's window, so Eye opened the back door to see what the beam of light was. As soon as Eye opened the door there were five police officers in my driveway with their guns drawn. Eye wasn't nervous or scared because Eye wasn't about to make any sudden moves or give them a reason to shoot. One of the officers said, "Come outside with your hands up." Eye let them know that Eye wasn't armed and Eye came outside and laid on the ground with my arms stretched out. One of the officers came and handcuffed me. As soon as Eye got handcuffed Jerome bursts outside and begins telling the police that Eye threatened to blow his brains out and that my gun was in the trunk of my car. Eye didn't say a word as Eye looked at Jerome in disgust knowing that he'd go to the extreme to blatantly lie on me. The officer got the keys to my car, opened the trunk and retrieved the case where my gun was. Eye arrived to the police station and was being processed in. When the detective looked at me as he was fingerprinting me he said, "Eye know one thing?" Eye responded, "What's that?" He said, "Eye can tell that your brother is a fucking liar."

For a moment there was a sigh of relief, but Eye was still being processed. Fourteen hours later Eye went before the judge and paid my own bail. My eldest brother Kurt picked me up and Eye told him what happened. A week later Eye went to court with my mother and Uncle Tom by my side. When we arrived at court Jerome was sitting with a few police officers busting it up as if he was an officer himself. The judge dismissed all charges and the prosecutor told me that Eye was free to pick up my firearm at the police station next door. When Eye got to the police station to pick up and sign for my weapon the Captain said, "Eye'm sorry that you had to go through this."

When Eye got in the car with my mother and Uncle my mouth was open but my spirit was speaking, "Jerome's going to lie on someone one day to the point it's going to cost them their life or freedom." Eye was focused more than ever to get away from this dude because wasn't anything good or positive happening for him and he was like a blazing tornado without a conscience.

In 1999, Eye moved to Florida because my job had a position opening and it would be a great distant away from the unnecessary drama that Eye was being pulled into. Finally, being free and able to advance my life into a new and better direction Eye began applying myself to explore different careers in the workforce. Eye was doing extremely well for myself.

In Dec. 2002, Eye just arrived to work and Eye received a call from Jerome. Jerome and Eye were very cordial up to this point because Eye really didn't trust him. Eye was a little nervous for a few reasons one was because it was still early in the morning and two, he never really had anything good or positive to say. Let's just say Jerome loved to be the "bearer of bad news." Eye said, "What's up Jerome?" He asked, "Are you sitting down?" At that point Eye knew it wasn't good, especially for him to make the attempt to give me bad or upsetting news. Eye responded, "Yes, Eye'm sitting down. What's up?" "Kurt was just framed for murder. The cops just picked him up from his home and taking him in for questioning. It's already on the internet." Eye immediately got off the phone and pulled up the information on the internet. You know Eye didn't trust anything Jerome said, so Eye had to validate the information. My heart seemed to drop to the bottom of my feet as Eye couldn't imagine what my parents were feeling. Eye made arrangements to take a leave of absence to be closer to my family during this time of emergency. Jerome was in touch with a mutual friend of ours that wanted to move up north. He and Jerome had an agreement, so Rick would end up helping me drive the distance. On the way, driving up north Eye stopped by to see my grandparents first. My grandmother said, "If Eye were you Eye'd wait it all out until his trial. Eye'm not going to tell you not to go because you're grown but you're doing so well for yourself and Eye don't want you to end up in trouble." My grandmother was extremely wise and Eye should've listened to her but the love Eye had for my family in spite of the differences kept me focused on leaving.

Rick and Eye make it up north and instead of going directly to my parent's house, we go straight to Kurt's home where Jerome would be waiting on Rick. Eye call my mother to let her know that we were in town. Eye decided to go through Kurt's mail to see if there were any past due bills so Eye could pay them before they lapsed. Eye began doing a little cleaning just to get my mind off of things. Eye drove to my parent's house to see if they were going to go visit Kurt but it wasn't a visiting day so the only people that could visit him was an attorney or member of clergy. Well, Eye was a licensed minister so Eye was able to visit Kurt. Eye knew what cops did to innocent people so it was up to me to make sure my brother was okay. Kurt told me that one of the detectives punched him in the face, but he didn't want to get all into that. Eye wanted to know what happened but Eye allowed his attorney to get all of that information. When Eye drove back to my parents Eye let them know that he was okay. Eye didn't bother to tell them a detective punched him in the face because Eye didn't want to add to them already worrying. Once again Eye became my brother's keeper, only this time it was my eldest brother. This was very puzzling to me because Kurt was a comedian, not a murderer. This was a defining moment because it showed Kurt who his true friends were and those that were only attached to him because of what he possessed or the things he had access to.

> *There's some people who YOU'VE ACCEPTED as a "Friend" that (1) Only became your friend to devour your character because they're jealous/ envious of your drawing power*

(2) are delusional into believing you want more than a friendship (3) are awaiting the correct moment to try and destroy what you're building (4) have become your friend because they THOUGHT you were part of a certain group, wanted to TRY you, but realized you were a horse from a different stable (5) are trying to become more than; to gain your TRUST, only to betray you (6) you've known prior to social media and they still have feelings for you and will also deny you, etc.

There's also people YOU'VE DENIED that (1) would've had your best interest at heart (2) is capable of being a true friend (3) would be a warrior on your behalf (4) could enhance your life/ lifestyle, etc.

POINT: Your life's experiences differ from that of the person YOU'RE CONNECTING with. YOUR interpretation, perception, or value may also differ! Time to evaluate and make the necessary cuts!! Kingdom/ Empire Building BEGINS with YOU!! - Lamont Bershawn.

The next morning my mother called and asked if Eye wanted to go to church with her, Eye really wasn't in the mood to go anywhere so Eye declined. Eye needed to get some air so Eye went to grab a few items from the supermarket. When Eye arrived back at the house one of Kurt's friends was there to see if it was anything they could do. Eye thought the gesture was nice because she was the first person outside of family that seemed to care. Jerome received a call later that day from the cousin of one of Kurt's "live in" friends. A "live in" friend, as Eye define it was actually a freeloader. The moment Kurt was arrested, the "live in" began stealing some of Kurt's valuables {jewelry, fur coats, money, etc.}. The cousin of the "live in" alerted Jerome that some of Kurt's valuables were over her house. Jerome was adamant

EYE'VE STOOD INSIDE THE EYE OF HELL AND REMAINED FEARLESS!

on retrieving Kurt's property, so he was looking forward to Troy {the live in} to show up. The phone constantly rang, but Eye allowed the answering machine to answer a few calls, anyone really important had my cell phone number. This one particular time the phone rang Eye decided to answer and it was Troy. Troy was very shocked to hear my voice and he asked, "what my plans were the rest of the day?" Eye told him who was at the house and we were planning on either going bowling or catching a movie. He wanted to know if he could join us and if Eye could pick him up. Rick, Jerome and Eye went to pick him up because we had to make a few more stops before going back to the house. We stopped by the mall to get an air mattress and then by the gas station. Eye thought everything was okay because we greeted each other with a handshake and everyone seemed to be in better spirits.

When we get in the house awaiting the ladies to return before we headed bowling Jerome punches Troy in the mouth. Jerome stands over Troy and asks him, "where the fuck is my brother's belongings? Eye know you have them because your cousin called me and told me." Jerome then pulls out a set of handcuffs and placed Troy's hands behind him and handcuffed him. He stood Troy up and walked him downstairs. Rick and Eye stood there in amazement looking at each other. When Jerome came back upstairs Eye asked him, "what the hell was all that about?" Jerome responded, "Eye want answers. Kurt opens his house to these people and they take advantage of him." Eye knew Jerome was hot headed and wasn't a logical thinker. It was at that moment Eye knew the devil himself was staging the atmosphere and it wasn't great. Too much was going on and my stomach started hurting, so Eye had to use the restroom. Rick was outside smoking a cigarette and Jerome was downstairs. The doorbell rang and Eye heard a woman's voice, Eye thought it was the people we were waiting on but it was Jerome's current girlfriend, Cecilia. Eye cracked the door open and all Eye could hear was Cecilia on her cell phone speaking with her girlfriend saying, "Troy is here, Jerome have him downstairs." In an instant Eye yelled for Jerome to come here. Eye was clean and out the bathroom by the time Jerome came upstairs. Eye pulled him in the room where Cecilia couldn't hear me.

Eye told Jerome to get downstairs and get Troy out of this house now. He responded shaking his head profusely saying, "okay." Jerome went and walked his girlfriend outside while giving her the keys to his car to drive. When Eye get downstairs Eye find that Troy is still there. Now the kicker was Jerome's girlfriend was Troy's ex-girlfriend. Damn! Can't he deal with someone that no one close to him dealt with?

Nevertheless, something spoke to me within my spirit and told me plainly to leave because this isn't the atmosphere you created. Eye disregarded the voice that spoke within my spirit. Eye went to the basement and saw that Troy was tied to a fucking chair and his braids were cut. The only thing that was hurt was his feelings. At that moment Jerome was trying to get a confession. Eye left from downstairs and Jerome and Rick followed behind me. The problem with that was Jerome still never untied Troy and he unknowingly left his cell phone beside him. When we got to the living room Eye blasted Jerome for doing dumb shit, yet Eye never left the house. Approximately five minutes later a rapid, hard and repetitive knock hit the door. Just by the sound Eye knew it was trouble for us. Jerome jumped off the couch and was about to run downstairs. Eye told him to sit his ass down, then Eye proceeded to open the door. It was four police officers. Eye asked them, "What's going on officer?" An officer replied, "We received a call that someone was being held against their will. Who's in the house? Eye told him exactly who was in the house from the top floor to the basement. Eye asked him if he had the correct address? He called out an address but it was the incorrect address, which gave me a second of a relief, then he gave the correct address.

One officer went upstairs, one went in the basement and two were in the living room placing us in handcuffs. Jerome identified himself as a school police officer to the Sergeant. When the Sergeant came upstairs he looked at Jerome and said, "Eye'm surprised at you." Here we are headed to the precinct to get booked on some charges. Once again, denying my spirit Eye found myself in trouble over some shit Jerome did. Eye thought to myself, "Eye should have let his ass continue downstairs and he'd have to answer to the charges alone."

EYE'VE STOOD INSIDE THE EYE OF HELL AND REMAINED FEARLESS!

We get to the police precinct and our attorney gets called to meet us there. We were being charged with simple assault. While we're speaking with our attorney The County detectives come in and extradite us {Rick, Jerome and myself}and transfer all charges to the County. Eye knew this wasn't good and some bullshit had taken place because this was the same place my oldest brother, Kurt was being held.

The next morning, we go before the judge for arraignment and it's the same bitch that Eye was in front of a few years back when Jerome lied on me. When she read the charges, there were ten more charges added to the simple assault. She gave us a bail of $500,000.00 cash, with the most serious of the charges being kidnapping. The prosecutors tried their best to link both cases together but they couldn't because their case was getting weaker by the moment. Here Eye am thinking, "What the fuck did Eye get myself into. My grandmother pretty much begged me not to come up here." To make a long story short, we stayed in the county jail for ninety-three days because our bail was lowered by the President judge to $100,000.00 cash. This was the most nervous Eye'd ever been in my life because Eye really didn't know what to expect. Eye looked back at my dad and he nodded which made me feel a little comfortable. When we left the court a few of the correctional officers said, "they're trying to railroad you guys, if Eye were you Eye'd sue the pants off this county." Well, that wasn't on my mind at the present moment, the only thing Eye could think of was getting the hell out of here. Do Eye take responsibility for my actions? Absolutely, without a doubt. Eye should have followed my mind or listened to the "VOICE."

Let's see if we've ever REALLY recognized the "VOICE!":

The "Voice" has many names {intuition, instinct, consciousness/ conscience, "God" within, Chi, inner man, power that be, etc.}.

(1) Have you ever been somewhere and the "Voice" spoke with you telling you to "Get the hell out of this place NOW?" {you listened only to find out something bad happened moments after your departure!!}

(2) Have you ever been driving and the "Voice" took you on another route, contrary to your normal way of travel? {later to find out you avoided a fatal accident!!}

(3) Have you ever ignored the "Voice" and found yourself in trouble? {happens daily with people}

(4) Have you missed out on a "Blessing" by following someone else's path instead of listening to the "Voice?" {of course}

(5) Have you and your friend ever been at a location and the "Voice" told you to "Immediately leave these premises?"

Your friend looked at your expression and dropped everything to follow you!!

{Your friend tells you Eye saw a look in your eye that ALERTED me. That was the power of discernment within your friend to recognize the power within you. Later to find out, the location you left was robbed and someone was murdered.}.

{The above are examples of coincidences that may have been a similarity in your life}

The "VOICE" is YOUR PERSONAL "SPIRITUAL GOD/ FORCE" that directs/ guides YOU!! The reason NOBODY else can hear the "Voice" that YOU hear is because it's designed distinctively for YOU. It's there to protect and guide you so RECOGNIZE IT, RESPECT IT and REACT/ RESPOND TO IT!!

We took a plea for simple assault and had everything else dismissed under our lawyer's recommendation. Eye knew this would be my very last straw of allowing someone to get me caught up in some mess.

Allow me to address the issue concerning Jerome's involvement with the School Police. Jerome never took the test to become a school police officer. He was real close with one of our former teacher's that worked as a Professor but was also a real police officer for the housing developments. He refused to get Jerome involved in the housing development police so he pulled a few strings to get Jerome a school police job. Jerome loved to be in authoritative positions and it went to his head. He really thought that (1) he was above the law and (2) he was a sworn officer of the law. Jerome worked that gig part-time and only while school was in. Jerome ended up getting fired from the school police because he was fighting students. It was probably best because he worked in a middle school and was making sexual advances to those young ladies. Jerome's girlfriend thought he was an officer of the law because he carried a gun and had a badge. School police officers don't carry firearms.

One weekend Jerome and his girlfriend were driving to North Carolina and he was pulled over for speeding in Maryland. When the officer asked for Jerome's identification instead of him giving the officer his driver's license Jerome presented his school police officer's badge. Two things wrong with this situation (1) he was just fired from his job and should have turned in his badge and the rest of his credentials {he was impersonating an officer} and (2) he had a loaded firearm in his vehicle. He ended up going to jail, losing his girlfriend and getting his gun taken from him. My mother bailed him out of jail and hired a great attorney that had a lot of pull, but he wasn't cheap. He ended up getting Jerome off, but he wasn't able to get his gun back and his now ex- girlfriend knew that he was famous for telling lies. Jerome seemed to stay in trouble and the best thing about all of it was Eye was nowhere around him.

> *"Learn to accept people for who they are and stop trying to accept them for the potential that you see within them. Some people will never achieve the potential or credit you're giving them because of the lack of internal wisdom, low self-esteem, or living in past hurts."*
> *- Lamont Bershawn.*

His friends began comparing him to me in more ways than one because they were truly beginning to see him for the person he really was. Once again, Jerome started hating me for the things his friends were telling him while making the comparisons. This was the defining moment that Jerome would cut me out of all of our pictures because he no longer wanted people to know that he had a twin brother.

My mother refused to give up on him although he cost her a lot of money. My dad wasn't getting involved in paying anymore legal fees for people that did stupid shit. Even after high school Jerome wanted to join the Army. Now that Eye think of it Eye'm guessing he saw himself as a complete fuck up and felt the need to get rehabilitated through military. Jerome went a signed up and Eye was happy for him, especially if that was going to give him a better sense of respect for himself. Eye'd never thought of joining the Army but my mother didn't want him to go in alone. Mom looked at me and said, "Please don't let him go in the military all alone because he's going to need a friend and Eye know you won't allow anything to happen to him." Eye told her, "He won't be alone because they'll be other people there for him to meet." My mother began to cry, so Eye signed to go in together on the "buddy team." Eye knew military wasn't for me but Eye did join to make my mother happy. Once again, "Eye'm acting as my brother's keeper."

A few months in my moral begins to get low and Eye no longer have the desire to be there. Eye walk up to the platoon Sergeant and tell him, "Eye don't even feel like being here any longer." Let me be honest and say, "Jerome and Eye knew about camping because my parents taught us how to survive the outdoors. My mother took us camping and my dad got us involved in hunting at the age of twelve." We were infantry soldiers and they loved the outdoors no matter the temperature and we'd bivouac {camp without cover} for days. Hell, we were on the "buddy system", so Eye became smart and began thinking like a soldier should. In other words, when they had something hard designed for us Eye made it a little easier. Most drill sergeants were happy and pleased because we showed them some of our survival techniques. Jerome took that to a whole new level. Eye was

EYE'VE STOOD INSIDE THE EYE OF HELL AND REMAINED FEARLESS!

pretty much the quiet brother, but very observant. Jerome was the one that told people believable stories that became very interesting. One evening the military had movie night for the troops. The movie was "Total Recall" with Arnold Schwarzenegger.

The conversation between Jerome and the First Sergeant seemed to be one that the sergeant thought would inspire the entire platoon, so instead of watching the movie Jerome and Eye became the center of attention. The sergeant gave a brief introduction about the lives he thought we had and we took center stage. Jerome was a professional liar, so he did all of the talking. Jerome told these soldiers that he was in the movie "Coming to America" with Eddie Murphy as the "stunt double" during the stick fighting and that Eye was the "stunt double" for Arsenio Hall. Jerome also told them that he helped choreograph Berry Gordy's "The Last Dragon." Oh, it didn't stop there because the great thing of it all was we actually did know martial arts, so we did a few demonstrations which got us over the hump and they believed the fabrications.

In the end Jerome took a few questions as to why we'd leave such a great life and join the military? Jerome said, "to fight for this great country in which we live." The next question, "What kind of car do you drive?" Jerome responded, "A 300sd turbo diesel Mercedes." We received a standing ovation as we exited the stage. We came home for the holidays and when we returned Eye knew that Eye no longer wanted to be in the military. The sergeant asked me, "do you still want out?" Eye responded, "absolutely." It was a few more weeks before graduation and my sergeant got word to the Colonel. On graduation day, Eye went before the Colonel. The Colonel said, "It's not my intention to keep a man in the military against their God given will. Eye don't know why recruiters tell people lies in order to make a quota. It is hereby ordered on this date that you are released from all duties as an active duty soldier in the United States Army. Thanks for your dedication soldier, good luck on your journey." Six months later, Eye received my Honorable Discharge from the United States Army.

Jerome began telling people that the only reason Eye was released was because Eye was suicidal, but what do you expect from someone that enjoy telling lies? Once again Eye was free from feeling obligated to allow people to see the liar Jerome was and it wouldn't have any bearing on me because we looked alike. It became tiring and Eye was getting exhausted of him thinking that Eye followed him places but more exhausted of people considering us the same because we looked alike.

"When you look in the mirror what are you seeing? "IF" you don't like what you're looking at, you have the power to change it. Once you begin to really appreciate your exterior, your interior will begin to change. Your reflection speaks volumes!! The greatest story ever told is NOT that of Jesus, but it's the one that's being written as you're living your OWN life!!"

----> **THE LIVING WORD** <--- Lamont Bershawn.

SHEDDING SOME LIGHT!!

Eye constantly hear people accuse myself and others of spreading "False" doctrine. Allow me to explain to some of you indoctrinated ass people EXACTLY what this means, since you'd rather sit in church and refuse to STUDY TO SHOW YOURSELVES APPROVED UNTO YOUR GOD!!

Let's define doctrine. According to the online dictionary doctrine is defined as a particular principle, position, or policy taught or advocated, as of a religion or government.

Do you see the words "Taught" and "Advocated" {to speak or write in favor of; support or urge by argument; recommend publicly}. In other words, whatever rules, laws, regulations, dogma, principle, discipline that your church, organization, belief system that's a part thereof; ANYTHING going AGAINST or is NOT mentioned in the system YOU "Be- LIE-Ve" will be considered FALSE.

Does it mean that because it's NOT in the religious beliefs that YOU follow, that it's "False" doctrine? ABSOLUTELY NOT!!

EYE'VE STOOD INSIDE THE EYE OF HELL AND REMAINED FEARLESS!

It just means (1) you have not learned of it as of yet (2) You are a closed minded individual {not willing to learn more information, but comfortable "knowing" what you have in your mind} (3) have a LIMITED perception (4) Have made the system you're a part of a "God" and therefore have enslaved yourself by conforming to a religious practice that have NOTHING to do with God/ Creator (5) You've spoken/ judged someone out of PURE IGNORANCE, etc.

When following religious doctrine according to the groups: 33% {Christians}, 21% {Muslims}, 13% {Hindu}, 6% {Buddhist}, 15% {Atheist} and 11% are {TOTALLY CONFUSED ABOUT ALL OF IT}!!

Why do Christianity hold more weight than any other religion? It's because Christianity is a manmade religion that's a conglomeration {to form or gather into a mass or whole} of ALL religion combined.

Whatever religion YOU follow or book YOU abide by someone in there said, "LEARN." It would be wise to "LEARN" prior to making judgments against someone that refuse to follow the curriculum that you choose to follow or live according to. "In all the information you're receiving, remember to receive an understanding!!"

When my first book, "Bishops Need Love Too" was released Eye received 4.75 stars out of 5 with twenty-five reviews. Eye released the book under a pseudonym under the advice of my publisher to protect everyone's identity including my own. It was one of my greatest accomplishments achieved but Jerome became jealous, irate and envious. He decided to write a review to attack my character but Eye wasn't bothered because it was expected. Eye began seeing women that were rejected by me because they had psychological issues, women that still carried grudges because they didn't go to my prom with me, women Jerome tried to hook me up with but weren't my type and women that disliked me because my religious views differed from theirs on Jerome's team. Eye realized that these women weren't really upset with me, they just wanted my attention and thought by getting closer to Jerome they'd receive it. Eye knew they really had no interest in dating him because they knew he had a passion for looking at naked men, at least that's what one of his ex- girlfriends said. Eye asked her was that the reason she decided to break things off, but she never responded. Jerome was an opportunist among other things. It didn't matter what the situation might be or consisted of, even if he had to deny his friends. Jerome had a friend that loved to sing and he called Jerome to let him know that God told him to tell Jerome that he could no longer be his friend. What this friend didn't know was that Jerome put in a bid to use him to get next to the millionaire he introduced Jerome to. It meant that Jerome had to plant negative seeds in the millionaire head and slander his name. Jerome asked me to talk to his friend because he was hurt that he no longer wanted anything to do with him. Eye told Jerome he needed to understand what loyalty means. Jerome would've never been introduced to the millionaire if it weren't for his friend.

"As you browse through your "Friends" list trying to figure out their nature, intention or motive; understand that they may not be an enemy, but an opportunist.

An opportunist is an individual that sits dormant awaiting the chance to use you as leverage for the purpose of gain or will wait for the opportune time to crumble your foundation. Their intention or goal have risen beyond infatuation. It's more of a "Fatal Attraction" or an "Obsession."

These individuals have been lurking in the shadows watching and critiquing your every move. You've become their study, their project, their "ace in the hole." You've been plagiarized and your patent have been copied, but you have yet to receive your royalties or credit for your creativity."

POINT: We connect to people all of the time. A connection can be for the purpose of networking/ business, spiritual reasons, sexual

EYE'VE STOOD INSIDE THE EYE OF HELL AND REMAINED FEARLESS!

desires {let's be real...lol}, religious affiliations, etc. When opportunity knocks, is it always beneficial for you or could you be opening the door to your demise? - Lamont Bershawn.

Most people would probably be asking, "why did Eye continue being a true brother to Jerome even though he had no good intentions towards me?" Eye'd try my best to please my mother because Eye knew what Eye saw her go through. The last thing she needed was to see her children at odds with each other. Eye'd give Jerome chance after chance to get his life in order, but each time it failed. When my first book was released Eye received a message on facebook from this lady named, "Alicia." Alicia said, "she wanted to push my book and become a business partner with me. Eye gave her my phone number and we began talking about business. It seemed that Alicia had her shit together and was extremely serious. Eye mean she began emailing me her business plans, her bank statements and telling me her vision concerning marketing me. To be honest, Eye was blown away because no one had ever been this upfront with me concerning business. She told me that she lived outside of Atlanta. Eye went to Atlanta to visit "Doc" and arranged a meeting with Alicia. We met up at the food court at one of the malls so Eye could autograph her book and talk business. We probably talked for an hour and then Eye treated her to a smoothie and we hugged and went our separate ways. Later that evening Alicia called me and asked had Eye given her business proposition any thought. Eye said, "Sure, Eye'd love to do business as long as we can keep it on a professional level." She responded, "Of course." Alicia said, "This calls for a celebration. Let's celebrate before you leave town." Eye asked Alicia, "What do you have in mind?" The day before my departure Alicia treated me to Arizona's restaurant.

We never signed any contracts just agreed to do be business partners. Eye got home and began receiving all kinds of gifts in the mail {flat screen television, clothes, candy, cereals, sodas, etc.}. It was as if Eye'd receive a box from Amazon every day. Alicia was taking frequent trips to see me about business, but Eye knew she began liking me more than what she was saying. She got in touch with a chemist to create my very own fragrance and she also had a book signing without my knowledge. Eye realized that she really didn't want a business together, she liked me or was so infatuated with me that she felt as if she could buy me. Eye let her know that Eye wasn't for sale and that she wasn't my type. Here we go again, another chic that was carrying the wounds from her past. She was so tired of being rejected by others that she felt the need to get men to be attracted to her by buying them material items. She contacted Jerome and they began talking, going out and frequently seeing each other. Eye guess they thought it would bother me, but Eye knew they were best for each other. Two bipolar, habitual liars and vindictive people with the same desire. Nevertheless, people especially Jerome's friends were seeing his true colors and recognized that Jerome and Eye are polar opposites.

When things become this close and coincidental one must learn to say, "Whatever!"

Sometimes in life YOU have to get yourselves to the point that you're saying, "WHATEVA" {whatever}!

When you're doing all you can do in a relationship/ marriage, on a job, in your church and you're still NOT appreciated - WHATEVA!

When that bipolar bitch delete or block you from FB, because they don't want you to know the negative things they're saying about you- "WHATEVA!"

When that friend of yours entice your other friend to talk about you for sexual reasons - WHATEVA!

When that church leader wants to include you in their sermons - WHATEVA!

EYE'VE STOOD INSIDE THE EYE OF HELL AND REMAINED FEARLESS!

> *When that jealous, insecure and envious person do ALL they can to destroy your reputation - WHATEVA!*
>
> *When people still want to keep your mind in a "Remember when/ Used to" state - WHATEVA!*
>
> *When your loved one, parent, or someone you thought cared for you or had your best interest at heart, tells YOU that "You'll never be shit!" {Thank YOURSELF}, but WHATEVA!*
>
> *When your ex is still upset you rejected them and they feel that getting involved with your former best friend or next of kin will bother you - WHATEVA!*
>
> *You have got to get to the point that your SELF PERCEPTION is NON-NEGOTIABLE!! So "WHAT THE FUCK EVA!!"*
>
> *POINT: Your destiny, Your character, Your belief, Your life, Your next moment is in YOUR hands. Don't allow people's jealousy, envy, or perception of YOU alter Your belief in Yourself. You must release the trivial or frivolous things in Your life and STOP ALLOWING them to reside within your spirit!! - Lamont Bershawn.*

This is just a portion of the things Eye had to deal with concerning Jerome, but Eye totally understand that Eye must be a protector of my own, and in doing so Eye can't afford to be my brother's keeper.

> *In all of my years on Facebook Eye NEVER had to defend my character or my name.*
>
> *It has gotten to the point that Eye refuse to allow anyone to disrespect me or my family.*

Here's the issue: A few years ago (2013) Eye wrote a book that was very controversial yet enlightening. One of my "supporters" from Facebook loved the book so much that they wanted to extensively market it.

To make a long story short we met up at the mall in Atlanta. She said that she could relate to my book in so many ways that she felt the need to help me brand it.

Let me be clear, Eye NEVER asked her for ANYTHING!!

Out of the blue she bought me a flat screen television, computer, clothes, jewelry and got a chemist to create my own fragrance. She flew out of town to meet up with me and asked, "how did you like the gifts?" Eye responded, "You can have all of it back because Eye don't want you to get the wrong idea about me." She responded, "I'm no Indian giver."

She began showing me her bank accounts as if Eye was supposed to be impressed. Later that week, Eye received a message from her ex-husband saying, how ungrateful Eye was for not showing up to my very own book signing. Little did he know Eye had no clue of any book signing on my behalf. Eye contacted her and told her that it would be in my best interest never to do business with her. She became upset and that's when Eye realized that she was bipolar, crazy and a basket case. She began crying, saying she loved me and telling me how she felt the need to buy love. Eye felt like Martin in a thin line... in a real life fatal attraction. Months passed by and Eye thought everything was over until she popped up at my door unexpected. Then Eye called my brother Dr. T and he told me that she attempted to do the same thing to him. He agreed with me that she needed psychological help. Eye rejected her and told her that she wasn't my type yet she wouldn't stop. She wanted to be vindictive so she tried dating my twin brother. She called me one final time telling me she was about to kill herself because she had nothing to live for because Eye refuse to even talk with her. Eye immediately hung up because Eye didn't want any part of that. When that failed she contacted my oldest brother who received double life for an alleged murder and ended up marrying him in July, 2017.

Eye'm serving notice on you "b.i.t.c.h." (Broken Individual Trying to Cause Havoc). You've been warned!!

In CONCLUSION: BYE ALICIA!! – Lamont Bershawn.

HE LEFT HER FOR DEAD

Forty-nine years she faithfully stayed by your side,
But all you wanted to do was run and hide,
Disrespecting, discounting and degrading her was all you did
Which ultimately gave your oldest son a double life bid.
Eye thought you wanted what was best for us,
Instead what you desired was a life full of lust.
You shady, cunning and slick motherfucker,
You wanted me to grow up being one of your suckers.
You only kept friends that would kiss your ass,
Constantly leaving my mother crying, praying and hoping you'd do better,
Eye'm the one sealing this final love letter.

You left her for dead one time too many
The millions you have...
Did you bother to give her any?
You wanted her to beg or struggle with the thought of her needing you,
She never once considered you "Little boy blue."
The prostate cancer made it impossible for you to get an erection,
Which forced your stupid ass to pay for affection.
Former Pastor, Eye've decided to throw the towel in,
Hell, Eye'd rather respectfully destroy you with this pen.

EYE'VE STOOD INSIDE THE EYE OF HELL AND REMAINED FEARLESS!

Over the years' you made some of your siblings hate her,
You were so close to one...
Fuck it Eye thought you dated her.
Co-signing for shit while neglecting your wife,
Never forget my nigga, THAT woman gave me life.
She did all that she could with the little she had,
Made me wonder all my life...
Eye forgot you're my dad.
You could never be my father,
You showed no love,
When Eye think about things neither did your father,
Makes me question, "Did he make it above?"

If Nana could see you she'd say, "Son stop dipping",
Eye'm sure your response would be "Mom, I'm just pimpin'."
It's a way of life that's just not new to me.
You just don't get it but Eye want the whole world to see.
Why Eye refuse to go to church every week and worship your deity,
The way you treat my mom...
You see clearly why your God don't mean shit to me?
As Eye put down this pen and lay things to rest,
Eye'm going to do my damnedest to become the very best.

Yeah you left her for dead...
But you loaded your gun with the improper lead,
Probably because your used to thinking with the wrong head.
Over forty years she dealt with your shit,
Finally, she decided to call it quits.
My mother she'll always be,
You disrespect her,
You disrespected me!!

By: Lamont Bershawn {Original piece}

It all began in the year of 1968, when Harry and Janice were united in "Holy Matrimony." The first few years were pretty good, Harry started working for the utility company after being Honorably Discharged from the Air Force. Janice at the time was a Licensed Practical Nurse {LPN}and also did home healthcare for the elderly. Two years into the marriage a son was born and two and a half years after that a set of twins were born. Janice did everything she could to raise us up with "Christian" values. Eye mean we went to church daily and it kept us out of trouble for the most part.

Allow me to start by letting you know the background of Harry and Janice. Harry came from a middle class, nine to five working family where everyone pretty much started working for the major utility company because Harry's father had been there for years and had enough clout and respect to get them in. Harry's father was married to Louise and from this marriage came seven children. Harry followed after his dad's footsteps in more ways than one. He saw his father disrespect his wife of many years by lavishing outside women with gifts, dinner and vacations. He did all of this yet financially took care of his responsibilities as a father and husband. Eye'd say he kept a roof over their heads, food on the table, bills and gave Louise very little money so it could all be accounted for. Louise kept the children in church every week while Tommy {Harry's father} attended a different church.

Janice came from a middle- class family that knew what it was to create their own businesses, they were entrepreneurs. Janice's father was the founder of his very own ministry and her mother helped him build, brand and market the ministry. They built several churches on the east coast from New York to Miami.

In the beginning of the marriage, Harry and Janice were happy and made a vow to keep one another happy. They also agreed never to depart each other angry or upset, go to bed mad or disavow each other or the marriage. Being rooted and grounded in the church Janice took her vows to Harry very serious. Harry on the other hand followed in his father's footsteps. Harry saw his father quite a few times out with different women, while his mother was the home keeper.

EYE'VE STOOD INSIDE THE EYE OF HELL AND REMAINED FEARLESS!

Harry and Janice lived in a middle-class neighborhood where there were "complete" families around. Eye mean there were a mother, a father and at least two children per household. It was a street where children were respectful and one or both parents had a profession {police officer, electrician, state trooper, lawyer, nurse, etc.}. Every parent on the block were able to get along and were able to "correctly chastise" every child doing wrong in order to keep them on the right path. It was a time when a child wouldn't get into "grown folk" business. We only knew what was going on in our own homes and no child would tell the other personal information about their household, in fear it would get back to their parents or to make it seem as if their family had it all together.

As a child having two other siblings in the house to talk to was easy, especially when we were on one accord and agreed. Eye recall one evening Janice was in the kitchen preparing dinner because Harry was on his way home from work. Jerome, Kurt and myself were in the room talking. Kurt assembled Jerome and myself because he wanted to confront Harry about mistreating Janice. When Harry got home and situated Kurt approached him and asked, "if it was okay to talk with him because there was a lot laying on his heart?" Harry responded, "What is it you want to talk about?" Kurt asked Jerome and myself, "Do you both agree with me?" We responded, "Yes." {Of course, we're going to agree with our oldest brother}. Harry took a seat at the head of the dining room table and folded his arms. Personally, Eye knew the conversation wouldn't end well. Kurt sat at the other end other table while Jerome and Eye sat in the middle chairs. Kurt looked across the table at Harry and said, "I'm tired of you disrespecting and mistreating my mother. Brittany wasn't enough! You don't think we didn't know about you sleeping with that woman in New York?" Harry immediately interrupted Kurt and said, "I'm grown!" Janice walks out of the kitchen and says to Kurt, "Kurt your father and I have already discussed this situation." Kurt says, "Nah mom, it's more to the situation and you need to know. I'm tired of seeing my mother cry because of your infidelity." Janice then says, "dinner is ready. Go ahead and wash your hands so you all can eat." Kurt says, "I'm not hungry anymore" {he proceeds to walk away and head upstairs}. Harry was already pissed and wanted a reason to hit Kurt. Harry looked at Kurt and said, "Your mother asked you to wash your hands so you can eat." Kurt replied, "I'm not hungry." Harry and Kurt began to tussle and Kurt sat Harry down in the chair. Harry got upset and slung Kurt into the glass table breaking it and the lamp. They began tussling again and Kurt ran upstairs and jumped under the bunk beds where Harry couldn't reach. Everything simmered down a few hours later and Janice attended to Kurt's cut on his back.

The next morning, Jerome and Eye went into Kurt's room and discussed the event that had taken place the night before. Kurt said, "I hope she leaves him." Knowing how strong Janice's faith is in God, Eye knew that wouldn't happen. Needless to say, Harry never stopped being a whoremonger and Janice accepted being mistreated and neglected.

Eye had a conversation with my Uncle about a few things, since he's a Christian Pastor.

Most Christian preachers do their best to either defend their "God" or make unreasonable excuses that don't make any sense whatsoever.

Me: Hey Unc. how's it going?
Uncle: Hey bookend {calls me that because Eye'm a twin}
Me: Can Eye ask you a question concerning the "God" you teach/ preach about?
Uncle: Sure. What's the question?
Me: What type of relationship did "God" have with his "son" Jesus?
Uncle: God loved his son unconditionally. As a matter of fact they were one.
Me: So, are you saying they were the same person?
Uncle: God was spirit and Jesus was the flesh of the manifested word.

EYE'VE STOOD INSIDE THE EYE OF HELL AND REMAINED FEARLESS!

Me: How so? When Jesus clearly let everyone know on several occasions that "he" prayed/ spoke to his father who is in heaven.

Uncle: {begins praying aloud} Father in heaven please give me the knowledge to deal with my nephew...

Me: If "God" loved his "son" unconditionally what was the purpose of the sacrifice {if "God" has all power}?

Couldn't "God" make the people withdraw from crucifying "Jesus?" If not, what's the use of praying to a powerless, prideful and tantrum having "God?"

Would you sacrifice either one of your sons?

Uncle: One of them I would

Me: You and my dad are the best examples of "Christians" that Eye've ever met.

Uncle: Well, that's very noble of you to say... Thank you nephew!

Me: Have you any clue as to what Eye just said? Do you understand what that means?

Uncle: Explain it to me because I'm not comprehending it.

Me: You two are the best examples of living the "Christian" life.

(1) Just like «God» didn›t «love», respect or give a damn about «his» only begotten «son» but shows favoritism to others. Reminds me of you two.

(2) Just like «God» wants to be worshiped. You two expect the same thing.

(3) Just like «God» expects to be placed on a pedestal... if not you›re quick to deny them certain rights and privileges

> *Nowhere in that bible did «God» and «Jesus» have a fruitful or loving relationship. «Jesus» always honored «God» and gave him credit. The average reader or pew dweller wouldn't ever see this truth, because they're too busy making excuses for "God" out of fear.*

> *Uncle: Well, your dad and I aren't perfect. Maybe that's why our prayers sometimes go unanswered.*
> *Me: Have you ever given it any thought that the reasons why your prayers aren't answered is because you're praying to something that don't have any real power?*
> *Uncle: My God has all power in his hands*
> *Me: If you say so. Quick question. Was your father a hoe?*
> *Uncle: {caught him off guard} huh? Yes, he dealt with lots of women.*
> *Me: Now Eye get it. Eye see why you and my dad sit in the church every Sunday.*

What Eye've learned is that religious people are quick to make excuses for their "God." It's as if they're really afraid to deal with their reality but would rather accept the fantasy through the biblical story. Since my Uncle is a Pastor, Eye gave him a scenario and asked him to explain it to me.

SCENARIO:

> *A young man proposes to his longtime girlfriend, she accepts. A few months later before they announce the wedding date, she drops a MAJOR bombshell on him.*

EYE'VE STOOD INSIDE THE EYE OF HELL AND REMAINED FEARLESS!

> *She tells him that she's pregnant, but he's NOT the father. He asks, "If I'm not the father, who is?" She begins crying and say, "Your father is!!"*
>
> *He responds, "You mean to tell me that you've been having sex with my father behind my back?"*
>
> *She begins to breakdown even more and says, "I'm not sure if your father or my father is the father of my baby." Shocked as all get out, he screams, "Incest!!!!"*
>
> *My questions to you are (1) Who is at fault? (2) What would you do?*

My Uncle responds, "she was wrong for sleeping with his father and her father after accepting the engagement proposal. If I were her fiancé I'd leave and never look her way again.

Hey Unc. Wouldn't that be wrong to do without forgiving her? Remember your "God" is a forgiving "God!"

Now allow me to give you the actual story so you can apply your belief system to it.

Actual story:

SCENARIO:

> *A young man {Joseph} proposes to his longtime girlfriend {Mary}, she accepts. A few months later before they announce the wedding date, she {Mary} drops a MAJOR bombshell on him {Joseph}.*
>
> *She tells him that she's pregnant, but he's NOT the father. He asks, "If I'm not the father, who is?" She begins crying and say, "Your father is!!"*

He responds, "You mean to tell me that you've been having sex with my father behind my back?"

She begins to breakdown even more and says, "I'm not sure if your father or my father is the father of my baby." Shocked as all get out, he screams, "Incest!!!!"

^^^^^ {This is the biblical story of Joseph, Mary and God "The Father."} If "God" is the Creator then {he- gender} is both of their father's, correct? So, "HE" being both of their father's acts as a Single, yet collective concept.

No wonder, why so many people get confused and emotional with the story.

My Uncle had no response of course.

Why did it seem that this family was falling apart? Why was it so evident that Harry no longer wanted to be married to Janice? Why did Harry hate me so much? Why was it so easy for Harry to support everyone except his immediate family?

One particular evening {Eye'll never forget} Janice parents came over for dinner. Eye don't know what took place after dinner but my grandparents engaged in a conversation with Harry. All Eye heard Harry say was, "if I didn't have them I'd be able to live like a king." My grandmother was the type of lady that wouldn't bite her tongue, especially when it came to her grandchildren. My G-mom responded, "who are you referring to motherfucker? If you don't want my daughter or grandchildren here I'll buy them a home tomorrow and dare you to go there." Now things were coming to a head. Harry was tired of dealing with Janice and he regretted having children with her. This is why Harry considered Brittany his "love child." Harry hated me even more because Eye became closer to my mother and acted as her protector. Years later Eye found out that all of his children were included as a beneficiary EXCEPT me and Janice in the event that something would happen to Harry. Eye never said or did anything wrong to him but was the one that would buy him expensive birthday gifts. Every gift Janice gave Harry over the years he gave back to her.

Harry began leaving Janice for a month at a time. During this time Harry never called to check on Janice, never left her any money and knew that Janice had doctor's appointments along with medication that made her feel ill. Eye called Janice everyday to check on her and send her money if she needed it. Approximately a month passed by and Eye asked Janice, "have you seen or talked with Harry?" She said, "No, he's been gone thirty-three days and I haven't heard from him at all." Eye asked, "how many times has he left like this?" Janice said, "this is the third time, but it's okay." Eye was in Atlanta helping my buddy operate his club, but it was something in her voice that Eye heard that helped me make the decision to get there. Jerome was on his way to Atlanta to help with the fairly new club and that was an extra added que to make me leave. Jerome and Eye can't ever do business together because he's not business savvy and besides he's a thief.

Eye left Atlanta and headed to take care of my mother. When Eye got home it was evident that Harry left her for dead. Eye told Janice three times gone for a month at a time is enough time for him to make settlement elsewhere. The mail was piling up but Janice never took care of the house bills so she was stuck. The only bill that Janice handled was the phone bill. A few weeks later, Harry entered the house and was shocked to see me there. We spoke to each other but Janice had gone bowling. Eye went back to my room to finish a few things and the doorbell rang. When Eye came downstairs to answer the door, Harry asked me was I expecting someone? Eye said, "no." Eye said whoever it was is walking across the grass. The backdoor bell rang and Harry said, "I'll get it, it's for me." Eye went upstairs and looked out the back window. It was Harry's mistress. Harry answered the door and the lady said, "you mean to tell me that you moved me up here for this. I'm going to let your wife know that I'm your new woman."

Later that evening, Eye spoke to Harry and told him that Eye didn't want anything to happen to Janice because he's slipping. Eye'm not sure what arrangement you have with this woman and Eye'm not sure what you told this woman but she was adamant about coming here where your wife, my mother resides. Luckily Eye was able to get the make, model and tag number of her vehicle so my mother could put a restraining order in place.

Forty-nine years married and a child outside of wedlock eleven years after the wedding and three children equals thirty-nine years of Hell to deal with. Harry left Janice for dead on several other occasions, but it's fit for my next book.

Why Eye Didn't Get Married

My first book, "Bishops Need Love Too" was published June 26, 2013. Eye remember FedEx arriving at my door early afternoon for me to sign for the package. Eye was so excited to finally see the finished product. Inside the package was one hard back and one soft cover book. Eye immediately posted it on Facebook to let people know my book was ready to be purchased. It wasn't a surprise to me that everyone wasn't going to support it because not everyone has your best interest at heart, sad to say not even those with the title of parent.

> *"Just because they have a title of parent don't mean they want the best for you in life!"*
> *– Lamont Bershawn*

My mother, Janice was extremely happy and proud but my dad, Harold despised me. Harold was the type of dad that was disrespectful towards us to get his point across. He hated me because Eye was my mother's protector and took sides with her because he'd always find a way to mistreat her.

> *"It's a son's duty to always look out for his mother, even when her husband doesn't." –*
> *Lamont Bershawn*

Eye was literally afraid of getting married because Eye never wanted to get involved in it and end up getting a divorce or separated. Eye knew all too well what marriage consisted of and Eye also knew that we were two individuals coming together from two different upbringings, lifestyles and experiences. Eye wanted to do the opposite of Harold when it came to respecting my wife.

Instead of teaching that a wife/ woman was the weaker vessel in the marriage. Eye was teaching:

> *HUSBANDS APPRECIATE YOUR WIVES. THERE'S NO WAY YOU COULD BE SUCCESSFUL WITHOUT HER.*
>
> *WHILE YOU HAVE "TUNNEL" VISION WHICH MEANS YOU MUST REMAIN FOCUSED, SHE HAS PERIPHERAL VISION WHICH MEANS THAT SHE'S CAPABLE OF SEEING YOUR SURROUNDINGS.*
>
> *YEP! THAT'S CORRECT, SHE EVEN SEES THE BANANA PEEL YOU'RE ABOUT TO SLIP ON, THE CUNNING ATTACK OF THE ENEMY, THAT BUSINESS PLAN THAT'S ABOUT TO TAKE A TURN IN THE WRONG DIRECTION AND EVEN THE INDIVIDUAL THAT'S DOING THEIR BEST TO DESTROY YOUR MARRIAGE.*
>
> *SHE'S STUCK BESIDE YOU BECAUSE SHE KNEW YOUR POTENTIAL, EVEN WHEN YOU HAD NO CLUE AS TO WHO YOU REALLY WERE. YOU'RE SUCCESSFUL BECAUSE SHE WAS ABLE TO "BIRTH" YOUR VISION INTO A SUCCESSFUL PLACE.*
>
> *YOU DARE NOT TREAT HER LESS THAN A PRECIOUS DIAMOND OR TRADE HER IN FOR CUT GLASS. IT IS SHE THAT WAS THE "WISDOM" THAT MADE IT*

EYE'VE STOOD INSIDE THE EYE OF HELL AND REMAINED FEARLESS!

POSSIBLE FOR YOU {THE HEAD} TO FUNCTION PROPERLY!!
BOW DOWN WITH HUMILITY, CHERISH HER PRESENCE AND HONOR HER ESSENCE!!
YOU COULDN'T HAVE DONE IT WITHOUT HER! – Lamont Bershawn.

When my first book, "Bishops Need Love Too" was released Eye received a call from a friend that this person was reviewing my book on Youtube and said it was a good read. It was another author promoting my book…WOW. Eye was amazed because Eye never asked her to do it but Eye've seen her share a few of my social media posts as well as did a blog on two of my posts. We began communicating as Eye wanted to really understand her views when it came to religion and the church. Candace told me she just got divorced and she was focusing on writing. Well, we learned we had a few things in common. We weren't talking much but when we did it was joyful because our conversations were hilarious. One day I was browsing and saw that something major wrong with her vehicle and it was costing her a lot of money so Eye messaged her to let her know if she purchased the part Eye'd install it for her. She thanked me and a few others on social media for the interest in helping her out. Candace called me and we talked approximately forty-five minutes and then she called me while she was on lunch. We had amazing discussions about any and everything. We became comfortable talking about anything until we realized there was a stronger connection we had for each other. We talked o the phone a month and then we became comfortable video chatting. Those chats were memorable because she recorded us singing, dialoguing and being our genuine selves with hilarious moments. When we decided that we'd finally meet each other Eye felt it was appropriate to detoxify our systems in order to physically remove the waste we were carrying sexually and spiritually cleanse our minds and spirits. One week before we met we detoxified our bodies. Candace actually drank her warm water and Epsom salt mix on video in front of me.

Many Christians have been searching for "Jesus" for years and have yet to find or locate "him."

They've been going to religious institutions praying, worshipping, crying and hoping that one day "he'd" show up.

All week long they've been "sinning" and feel the need to be cleansed.

The REAL "JESUS":

J- Just a cup of warm water with two tablespoons of

E- Epsom

S- Salt

U - Underwear because you're going to release every bit of

S - Shit in your system

GUARANTEED to cleanse your system and your "sins" away within a couple of hours!!

Forget the 10, 18 and 21 day taking pill cleanse.

Once you try this "JESUS" your life will never be the same.

Don't worry about "backsliding!"

Only need to be done TWICE a year {once every six months}.

Side Effects: Longer life, free of disease, trim waist, clean blood and bill of health!

Love you to LIFE!! – Lamont Bershawn.

EYE'VE STOOD INSIDE THE EYE OF HELL AND REMAINED FEARLESS!

On July 7, 2017, after speaking on the phone for two months Eye flew Candace out to Louisiana to join me in supporting Janice and her bowling team. My flight arrived there an hour prior to Candace but Eye rode the hotel shuttle to pick her up when she arrived at the airport. The moment we finally met we hugged each other as if we knew each other as if it had been years since we've seen each other. Candace was wearing a fitted black dress and Eye had on a pair of jeans with my alligator shoes. We sat on the shuttle heading back to the hotel holding each other's hand and then we passionately kissed each other as she relaxed and laid her head on my shoulder.

When we arrived at the hotel Candace freshened up and then we went to Janice room where she met the rest of my family. We went back to the room where Eye gave her a "money rose" that Janice made for her along with a personal writing from me and a music cd so she'd always remember that moment we shared together. It was a little late but we decided to make our way to the casino to play a little. We didn't win but we enjoyed each other's company. We stayed in the casino about an hour before we decided to get some rest.

Upon arriving back in the room, we got showered up and Eye put the cd Eye made on and we made passionate love all night long. The room was a little cold because of the temperature but Candace cuddled right next to me and we rested peacefully. The next morning, Eye awakened and walked over to the bowling arena while Candace slept a little longer. When she got up she met me over at the arena where we ate and watched Janice and her teammates bowl. Candace got along with everyone and seemed to be having a great time with me. The Sunday came and Candace was supposed to leave but she wanted to stay because we were taking a ride to New Orleans. Eye paid the difference in the cost of her flight and gave her One- hundred dollars because she ran out of money and Eye didn't want her to be broke being with me. We had a blast in New Orleans and Eye knew we only had one more day to spend together and we made the best of it. The next day we slept in spending as much quality time as possible. We went to the casino for an hour as the time was drawing near for her to leave. Eye asked Candace how much money did she lose while being with me? She said One thousand dollars and at that moment Eye handed her eleven hundred dollars and asked her to replenish her account. Candace looked at me and said, "No one has ever done this for me, thank you!" Eye replied, "Eye wanted you to enjoy yourself and go home feeling joyful, not miserable for losing money and wishing you'd never came." We held hands as we were riding back to the airport for her departure. She started crying saying, "She had such a wonderful time and that she didn't want to leave me." Eye said, "Don't cry, we'll see each other again real soon." Candace asked, "So where do we go from here?" Eye asked Candace, "What would you like to have with me? Candace replied, "I want to be with you, my last days to be spent loving you." Eye replied, "Are you telling me that you want a relationship with me?" Candace said, "yes, I want you as my husband." We embraced and kissed as she caught the escalator towards her gate.

When Candace got home she called me and let me know that she arrived safely and then she went on Youtube to make a video telling the world how she enjoyed herself. We had a great time making our personal video to Blackstreet's song, "Deep" and dialoguing openly on video. Eye had no clue that Candace was seeking so much attention from the world, Eye just thought she loved capturing the special moments in her life. Again, all Eye ever saw was the book review she put on video, Eye wasn't a follower of hers because Eye was too busy promoting my own book. Later that evening we talked about the amazing time we shared and didn't want to prolong seeing each other again. Immediately, Eye asked Candace to look at her calendar to see what her availability was in two weeks. Candace was free so Eye booked her flight to visit me in Pa. Candace was excited because now something was etched in stone as to when we'd see each other again. Eye began packing my things because Eye'd be leaving the next afternoon to fly home. When Eye arrived home and got settled Candace and Eye talked on the phone. We began video chatting from our laptops and phones so we could see each other. We laughed, joked reminisced about the time we just shared, talked about past situations, our books and future plans. Candace said, "I was serious about making you my husband. I never had anyone treat me like you did or make sure I was financially okay. I even told my mother the beautiful things that you said and did and mom even said that you're a rarity." Eye didn't do anything out of the norm. Eye was just being myself, but Eye guess she never experienced being with a gentleman.

My mother was preparing to drive to Florida in a week so Eye asked Candace was she free to fly to Florida next week? She was available so Eye paid for her flight and immediately emailed her reservation. Now we'd meet each other in Florida and the following week we'd be at my home. Continuing the conversation concerning marriage, Eye asked Candace if she was serious to set a date? Candace set a date for April 28, 2018. Eye agreed to the date and immediately shared the information with my mother. My mother thought that Eye was joking until she heard it from Candace via video chat. Eye asked Candace her ring size but she didn't have a clue what it was. Eye asked Candace to go to the mall inside a jewelry store to get her ring size. When Candace called me, she gave me her ring size and Eye took my mother ring shopping with me because Eye didn't want to get anything too gaudy. We looked at a few rings but the one that caught my Eye was a two-carat solitaire, Princess cut laid in a platinum setting. Eye purchased the ring and booked my flight to visit Candace the week after she'd come visit me.

Eye called Candace when Eye got home but Eye never let her know that Eye actually purchased a ring for her. Eye told her that, "Eye was going to do everything in my power to make this relationship work and try my best not to allow so much time get in between our visits." They say, "Absence makes the heart grow fonder" and Eye wasn't going to make any excuses from my end.

Mom and Eye drove to Florida, stopping briefly in North Carolina to meet up with Jerome and his fiancée Cathy as they trailed us to Florida to see Jerome's daughter and her new baby. Eye was pacing myself so that Eye had time to freshen up before driving to the airport to pick up Candace. Everything went as planned and now it was time for me to pick Candace up. Candace gets in the car and kisses me. We went to the hotel where we were staying to drop off her bags, so she could also freshen up then we headed back to my niece, Bobbi house. When we arrived, Eye asked everyone if they were hungry? The response was, "yes", so Eye treated everyone to a soul food buffet. This weekend in Florida was great for a few reasons:

The first time Eye get to see the new baby, he was turning three.
Candace would meet new family members.
My mother gets a chance to see me and Jerome being cordial.
Floyd Mayweather final boxing match.
Eye get to dress up as a Paw Patrol character for my great nephew.

Everyone enjoyed their time in Florida as it came time for Candace and Eye to depart once again. This time it wasn't so difficult to depart because we'd see each other again in five more days. When Candace got to Pa. we went to the casino to gamble a little. Eye knew she didn't have much money so gave her one hundred dollars to start and Eye went to play. We met up within the hour to see what we accumulated. She didn't win anything and my mother didn't win neither. Eye hit on a few different machines and put my winnings together which added up to seventeen hundred dollars. Eye gave Candace and my mother three hundred dollars each and said, "have fun." We left the casino and went to the hotel to rest up for the next day. When we got to the hotel, we ate a few snacks we brought, showered and went to bed.

The next morning, we awakened and went to breakfast. Eye called my mother to see what her plans were for the day and she really didn't have anything to do, so Eye asked her if she wanted to hang out with Candace and Eye for the day? My mother said, "yes." We rode out to Vanity Fair Outlet Mall because Eye wanted to buy Candace a few things that she needed. Eye bought her three bras and six pair of panties that she liked and could wear. Candace said, "she didn't wear panties or bras because she never knew her size." My first thought was how in the hell you don't know your size at the age you are? Then Eye had to realize that she paid for body enhancements and therefore probably wasn't interested in wearing anything.

LADIES AND GENTLEMEN:

PLEASE UNDERSTAND...

EYE'VE STOOD INSIDE THE EYE OF HELL AND REMAINED FEARLESS!

IT'S IMPOSSIBLE TO LOVE SOMEONE ELSE OR EVEN REMOTELY LIKE SOMEONE ELSE WITHOUT LOVING/ LIKING YOURSELF FIRST.

STOP TRYING TO PLEASE SOMEONE ELSE {ASS INJECTIONS, BREAST IMPLANTS, PENILE RODS, ETC.} PLACING YOURSELF ON SOMEONE'S TROPHY CASE JUST AS A SHOW PIECE.

IT REMINDS ME OF "THE WIZARD OF OZ" IF I ONLY HAD A...

SCARECROW {BRAIN}
TIN MAN {HEART}
THE LION {COURAGE}
DOROTHY {JUST WANTED TO GO BACK HOME}
THE WICKED WITCH {DOROTHY RUBY RED SHOES}
THE GREAT AND POWERFUL WIZARD {WANTED TO BE LIKED}

ONLY TO FIND OUT THAT EVERYTHING THEY EVER REALLY DESIRED WAS ALREADY INSIDE OF THEM AND NOT PREDICATED UPON ANOTHER.

THE WICKED WITCH CASE: SHE WANTED SOMETHING THAT DIDN'T BELONG TO HER AND ENDED UP DEAD.

THE WIZARDS CASE: HE ENDED UP BEING LIKED FOR WHO HE REALLY WAS INSTEAD OF TRYING TO BE SOMEONE ELSE.

POINT: REAL PEACE AND JOY COMES FROM KNOWING WHO YOU REALLY ARE!! DON'T END UP DEAD, DESIRING SOMETHING THAT WASN'T FOR YOU IN THE FIRST PLACE!! – Lamont Bershawn.

Candace was very happy and made a video for the world telling them how embarrassed she was that she didn't know her own size but she had a man that was in tuned and cared, so Eye was making sure she had what she needed. Eye wasn't trying to change Candace's lifestyle or put her in missionary church clothing, Eye wanted her to know that it wasn't anything Eye wasn't willing to do for her within my power. We had a very eventful and productive day and then we went to a restaurant to finally eat. Later that evening Candace and Eye began dialoguing concerning relationships, so that we'd have a better understanding of each other. Afterwards, Candace asked me if she could borrow five hundred dollars because she was a little behind in her bills. Immediately without question Eye let her borrow the money she needed. She felt so relieved that she began to cry saying, "I don't know what I would have done if you weren't in my life."

When we woke up the next morning we went to my mother's house and we made homemade apple dumplings and Eye cooked dinner before Eye dropped Candace off at the airport. Eye cooked venison {deer meat}, rice, broccoli bread with cream cheese and cheddar cheese and baked a 7up cake. Eye figured Eye'd surprise her and let her know that Eye can really cook. We talked all the way to the airport while Candace had her hand on my thigh. She began crying and said, "I seem to always do this when we depart each other. Eye told Candace, "stop crying sweetheart because Eye'm going to see to it that one day we'll never have to part ways." By the time Eye made it back home Candace had arrived at her gate. She told me, "she always consumes an alcoholic beverage prior to flying because it calms her down." Eye remember telling her to be careful because Eye didn't want her to be dependent on alcoholic beverages to the point it became an addiction. We video chatted with each other until she boarded her flight. When she arrived home, she called me and let me know that she arrived home safely and that she couldn't wait to see me the following weekend.

All week Eye was making preparations to propose to Candace. Eye went to my tailor to make me a suit with the accessories. Eye bought new cufflinks, tie and handkerchief for the occasion. Eye spoke with Candace that evening and asked her to gather her immediate family members for dinner at her favorite restaurant the day after my arrival. Eye made reservations at the Hard Rock Casino Hotel where we stayed my duration there since Candace was ashamed to take me to her home, but Eye didn't mind.

The next evening around six o'clock we began getting ready to meet up at Olive Garden. First Candace had on a black dress that was slightly shear. In other words, in light anyone could see right through it. Eye'm assuming she felt a little uncomfortable with it on because she changed without me saying a word. She changed into a more respectful black dress and that made me more comfortable with my decision to propose. Candace had no idea that Eye had a ring and was preparing to propose to her in front of her family. Eye felt that it was more honorable to ask her hand in front of her family. When we arrive at the restaurant her mother and two sisters are there. Candace's daughter and her boyfriend arrived thirty minutes later. We just finished eating when Candace niece walks in for a brief moment to formally introduce herself to me and before she left Eye said that Eye had a surprise. Our area was quiet for a moment while Eye said, "Eye know that Candace and Eye have known each other for a little time but it seems as if Eye've found my soulmate, my rib and the lady Eye desire to be by my side for the rest of my life. {Looking into Candace's eyes} Will you marry me?" Candace started to cry once again and said, "YES!" Everyone at the table began either hugging or shaking my hand congratulating us. We left the restaurant, went back to the hotel and made passionate love all night long.

Waking up the next morning still in disbelief that we're now engaged, Candace begins looking at the ring saying, "you definitely know how to make a woman have a heart attack in a great way." Eye replied, "when Eye felt it was right Eye knew Eye'd react and make it official. A few people knew that Eye was in town and Eye received a call asking to meet up later that evening. Candace and Eye met a few friends at the Marriott Hotel where a social meet and greet was going on. We danced, talked, took pictures and when the people found out that we got engaged the day before we received two complimentary flutes filled with champagne. Candace consumed more than she could handle and had to lean on me because she could barely walk straight. Luckily, Eye knew how to get back to her house. When we arrived at her house she began getting undressed while stumbling. Eye looked at her and said, "this is why Eye don't drink or get involved in relationships with women that can't hold their liquor or know their limit." Candace began crying and apologizing and said it will never happen again. Eye asked her, "why did she drink so much?" Candace replied, "because Eye saw those women all over you Lamont and this is what she was used to doing with men prior to having sex." Eye responded, "First of all, Eye'd never disrespect you with allowing women to be all over me. This is why Eye don't have sex with intoxicated women because Eye want them coherent and Eye don't want to be blamed for taking advantage of anyone." Candace apologized and we made love and cuddled the rest of the night.

The next morning Eye was supposed to fly home but Eye knew Candace wasn't in any position to drive me to the airport and Eye didn't want to call a taxi because Eye wanted to make sure Candace was in her right mind before Eye left. Eye stayed an extra two days which was good because Eye filled her refrigerator with food, bought her a television and unclogged her bathtub and sink that was full of hair and junk. When Eye'm in any relationship Eye see what needs to be done and help with whatever {laundry, fixing anything, cleaning, cooking, etc.}. Eye showed Candace who Eye was and what Eye was about and Eye never judged her for the things she did. Eye explained to Candace that we'd have a long lasting, healthy relationship as long as we were open and honest with each other. Eye wasn't concerned about her past and she wasn't concerned about mine because that was a point in our lives where we were at that moment. What Eye loved is that we had heart to heart conversations, great dialogue about relationships and the church. She was an ex- wife of a pastor and Eye used to be a pastor, so we used to laugh about some of the things that took place behind the scenes of church life. One day Candace began recording some of the things Eye said concerning the church and it received a lot of respect on social media. Candace lived for social media attention and validation, but Eye really didn't know the extent of it until later on.

EYE'VE STOOD INSIDE THE EYE OF HELL AND REMAINED FEARLESS!

"There's a price to pay when you make the world your stage!" – Lamont Bershawn.

Eye did everything that a man in a relationship would do for his fiancée, especially when he loves, respects and don't want to see her without. Candace felt a little embarrassed to tell me that her house was in litigation due to her brother in laws negligence. Eye understood exactly what she was telling me but what Eye didn't understand was, "where was her money going after she would get paid?" Candace worked as an insurance agent and was carrying life insurance on her mother, stepfather, first ex-husband, daughter, son, three granddaughters, herself and her daughter's boyfriend. When Eye found out Eye explained to her that was too much for her to handle, especially when it will only benefit you in the event of death. Candace understood what Eye was saying because one of her co-workers told her the same thing which confirmed what Eye was explaining to her. Eye was also wondering why we always went to the casino to eat on comps instead of her cooking. When Eye took her grocery shopping, Eye asked her to get the things that she could fix fast for lunch and things she would be good for a few days, this is what my mother would call a stretch meal. Candace said, "I don't have any money for groceries." Eye replied, "If Eye wasn't going to pay for your groceries we wouldn't have come here." Candace smiled. When we got back to her house Eye cooked stuffed bell peppers and she baked a "dump cake" in the toaster oven. Only two eyes were working on her stove, the oven part didn't work. Eye was going to buy her a new stove but she said that she usually goes over to her mother's house to eat a substantial meal or her sister would take her out periodically. She thanked me for being a tremendous help but Eye didn't always feel comfortable because her front door lock was completely broken and in order to fix it, she needed have it reframed. There were two brackets holding a long 2x4 piece of wood preventing people from kicking the door in. This is when Eye began questioning what she was actually portraying. Candace was more concerned with the way she looked opposed to her reality. She'd make sure her hair, nails, shoes and clothes were in tact but everything else was secondary, because she loved to take "selfie's" with her phone. Eye loved the fact that Candace would call her mother daily to check on her as Eye'd always call my mother to check on her as well. There's nothing Eye wouldn't do for my mother or my lady within my power. There were a few instances that my mother needed me to transfer money to her account and there were no questions being asked, Eye just did it. Actually, Eye'd send more than she need because my mother would only ask for the bare minimum in order to get by.

Candace heard me talking with my mother and when Eye hung up the phone Candace asked me if it Eye could let her borrow money to pay her cell phone bill, Eye paid it so her phone wouldn't be shut off.

> *"Y'all sistahs be sooo consumed with the ATTENTION u get on social media...*
> *"SEE ME? LOOK IM PRETTY...PLEASE LIKE ME!?"*
> *SHYT IS SERIOUSLY SAD...*
> *THE FACT THAT U NEED THAT PLASTIC ASS ATTENTION SHOWS A REAL MAN THAT U WILL NEVER VALUE THE ATTENTION HE GIVES...*
> *U FEEL OBLIGATED TO STAY IN THE MIRROR TAKING PICS HOPING FOR THE PUBLICS APPROVAL...*
> *WEN IN REALITY U DONT EVEN APPROVE OF URSELF...*
> *priorities fucked up...*
> *WAT U LOOK LIKE USUALLY NEVER WILL BE A DECIDING FACTOR AS TO WHY A KING EVEN CHOOSES U!"* –
> *Nawjaye Santiago.*

We were still on cloud nine because we're embarking on a new life together. Eye began taking my explicit photos down to honor my future wife, deleting/ blocking women Eye'd been sexual with from

EYE'VE STOOD INSIDE THE EYE OF HELL AND REMAINED FEARLESS!

my past and when phone calls came in from women from my past Eye'd let them know that Eye was engaged to be married and they respected that. Eye let Candace know what Eye was doing and she was amazed because no man she'd ever dealt with took the relationship that serious. Eye mean, from my perspective it was the correct thing to do to honor the lady Eye intended to spend my life with. This was my last night before taking flight in the morning so we began making our wedding party lists and the guest list. We began talking about colors and the type of wedding we were going to have. Candace's stepfather called her to see how she was doing and she told him that she just got engaged to be married. He was happy for her and wanted to meet me the next time Eye came to town for a visit. When Candace got off the phone we went to the casino for a couple of hours to get a bite to eat and gamble. Candace didn't have any money so she asked me if she could borrow five hundred dollars and she'd pay me when she got paid. Eye let her borrow the money because Eye wanted her to have fun too. When we arrived back at the house we showered and went to bed.

Candace dropped me off at the airport gave me a hug and kissed me before Eye checked my bags at the counter. Eye looked back and she was still out there watching as Eye waived and walked up the escalator. The flight was on time and Eye had a stop in Chicago so Eye called her when Eye got there. Candace said, "Eye can't wait until we no longer have to leave each other." Eye replied, "Eye can't wait neither." She then asked, "Am I enough for you?" "Absolutely", Eye responded. "Eye'm not sure what you went through in your previous relationships, but Eye'm not those individuals babe." Candace looked relieved. Eye looked at her and repeated what she asked me. Candace replied, "I never cheat, nor have I loved anyone as much as I love you. You're definitely enough for me, Lamont." "Do you love your engagement ring?" "Oh my God, YES! No one has ever given me a ring before." Huh? "In neither marriage?" {Candace holding her head down} "No." "How many times did you get married, Candace?" "I was married to the pastor for twenty-five years, one marriage wasn't ever recorded and I was married to Tyrone for five years", Candace responded. "You mean to tell me neither of them bought you a ring?"

"No, Lamont." "I've been through so much in my life and had given up on love until you came along and showed me something different than what I was used to. You flew me to places and paid for everything, bought me a number of things that showed you cared about me from the beginning. You took the time to listen to me and you allow me to voice my opinions. It's just the things you've said and backed everything up with action. No man has ever freely given me money just to make sure I had something in my wallet. You shocked my mind ever since Baton Rouge when you asked me how much money I lost and you gave me every dime plus an extra hundred. I don't want you to think its all about the money but you've done more for me in this short period of time than anyone has done in my entire life. All I can say is Lamont, Lamont, Lamont." Eye caught the second flight and headed home feeling a little sad about the information Candace shared. Eye wasn't doing anything out of the ordinary, Eye was just being me. This reminded me of the different perceptions of "love."

> *"A person's perception of Love is unconditional, bonding, romance, intimacy, etc. but you meet another individual who has been abused and knocked around all of their lives, have seen it in their parents, their friend's relationships, their cousins, etc. All that person knows as their perception of Love is what you consider abuse. The only thing that's designed is you through creation, all else you must design for SELF!!"* – Lamont Bershawn.

Eye was a little tired when Eye arrived home, but Eye took a shower and got ready for bed. Eye called Candace on video chat and she just finished editing a video of our engagement. Candace and Eye were talking and Eye asked her how long has she been divorced? Candace paused for a moment, so Eye thought she was thinking but she wasn't. Candace said, "I haven't heard from nor have I seen him in five years." "That wasn't my question Candace." Candace replied with, "I never filed the papers." Needless to say, that Eye felt like an ass. In my thoughts, I was engaged to someone still married which nullifies the engagement. Candace had the audacity to ask, "If you would have known that I was still married would you have proposed?" In an instant Eye responded, "HELL NO! What man in his right mind would?" Candace got in her feelings and started to cry. This time Eye told her to call me back when she got herself together. Candace called me back within ten minutes and apologized. She asked if we could sleep with our video chat on. Eye was okay with it. Eye mean it was a little odd or different but Eye guess so much has happened in her previous relationships when she felt they were upset they'd probably cheat, but Eye'm not that type of person. Deep down on the inside Eye felt as if Candace was deceiving me by withholding this information and felt there might be other things that Eye'd find out later concerning her, but Eye didn't slow up my personal momentum or interest in making her my wife. Eye felt that we could and would work through anything.

Here it is the middle of August, literally one month into our relationship and between us we've flown five times already, that's equivalent to a minimum of $2000.00 not including hotel. Eye did what Eye felt necessary to keep this relationship moving in a positive and progressive fashion. Eye have no regrets for the things Eye did because my heart was into Candace. We video chatted each other everyday and had deep conversations. Eye've literally been home a few days and during the vide chat Candace kept taking the phone away from her face. Eye asked her, "What's wrong? Why am Eye seeing the ceiling instead of your face? Are you falling asleep?" Eye didn't realize she was crying as if someone close just died. Eye asked Candace to look at me? Candace replied, "I filed the divorce papers and my ex-husband Tyrone contacted me and I'm afraid he's going to kill me? I always told my family if anything ever happens to me, Tyrone did it." Eye asked her if she was really that scared? She said, "yes." Eye picked up my laptop and made flight reservations to fly out to Candace the very next day. We continued to chat until she fell asleep. When she awakened for work the next morning Eye asked her to pick me up from the airport at six o'clock p.m.

When Eye arrived, Candace was waiting outside of baggage claim. Eye spent one week with her until she settled her fear of Tyrone doing something to her. While Eye was there Candace had to appear in court because Tyrone got a lawyer and was contesting the divorce because he wanted a portion of the money he thought Candace was due to receive. Eye stuck by her side every step of the way during this ordeal. The Judge gave her another date around the end of October because Eye was due to be back in town, so it was convenient that Eye didn't have to make another emergency trip.

When we were leaving the court house Candace began crying again saying, "we haven't seen each other in five years. Why is he doing this to me?" Tyrone's attorney approached us and Candace introduced her family to the attorney and said, "this is my fiancé, Lamont." The attorney spoke with Candace and asked her a few questions, afterwards she felt relieved because he told her if his research comes up empty then he's going to withdraw from the case. We left the court house and the nervous energy was gone so Candace could eat something. We rode out to Hard Rock Casino because we both had a free buffet. This particular trip a lot of signs were revealed that Eye paid attention to but didn't speak about all of them because Eye didn't want her to feel bombarded. I was in her room resting and she text me from her office. When Eye responded, she took my response the wrong way. Candace responded with "I quit." My reply to that was, "Eye quit too." Immediately, Candace came into the room where Eye was with tears in her eyes. Standing at the door she asks, "So, you don't want to be with me anymore?" Eye replied, "you gave me the impression that you no longer wanted to be with me." "Lamont, you're the air I breathe, you're my soulmate and I love you." Eye embraced her and held her tight saying, "Eye'm never going to leave you. Eye'm making countless efforts to allow you to see that it's all about you. There's no one else."

Eye began seeing empty bottles of water in the corner, under the bed along with four empty bottles of Vodka. Eye asked Candace, "why so many empty bottles of vodka and water?" Candace said, "I take a drink at times because I rest better." Eye responded, "so you take a drink of Vodka before you go to bed, a drink prior to taking a flight and used to drink prior to having sex with men. Do you consider yourself dependent or addicted to Vodka?" Candace got upset, "I'm not addicted to anything. Nothing is too hard for me to walk away from or drop." Part of me felt that she was upset and making reference to me, that she could drop me. Eye began seeing bottles of medication such as **Promethazine** *{an antihistamine. It is used to treat allergic reactions and to treat or prevent nausea and vomiting from illness or motion sickness. It is also used to make you sleep before surgery, and to help treat pain or nausea after surgery}.*

Promethazine is also an ingredient for "**Sizzurp**." The main ingredients in **sizzurp** are prescription strength cough syrup containing codeine and promethazine. The cough syrup or **sizzurp** is often mixed with ingredients like Sprite or Mountain Dew. Most often **sizzurp** is purple, hence purple drank, and the purple hue comes from the dyes in the cough syrup.

Sizzurp can cause respiratory depression which is potentially dangerous or even fatal. This effect of sizzurp is associated with the codeine in it which is an opiate. This makes sizzurp not only incredibly dangerous but also highly addictive. - {Bing definition}

Eye asked Candace, "why so many bottles of Promethazine. She told me it she took them after her "body enhancing" surgery. Candace said, "I gave them to my daughter's boyfriend. His family is into all those different types of drugs." This created a red flag for me because Candace did admit that she used to smoke marijuana with her daughter and her boyfriend. Candace had a sniffling problem, so Eye asked her, "had she ever snorted cocaine?" "She paused for a moment and said, "no" but Eye really didn't believe her. Eye think she told me what she thought Eye wanted to hear because she thought Eye'd judge her. Eye was involved with a woman that snorted cocaine, so Eye knew what to look for and Candace seemed to have it down. Eye wasn't ignoring the signs that seemed valid in my presence, Eye was taking notes. Eye'm thinking to myself, "if you felt comfortable doing that with your child what else have you done, but Eye didn't bother to ask." She also carried a lot of different color pills in her purse along with penetrating jellies used for sex and flavored sex jelly. That's when it dawned on me that maybe Eye'm not the only person Candace is being intimate with. Eye mean, Eye'm 1200 miles away and can't see through the phone. Many times, laying in the bed it seemed as if she was either dreaming or reminiscing about sexual encounters because she'd lightly moan and move her butt in a circular movement. Something had a hold of her that Eye couldn't explain, but Eye still loved her and wanted to marry her. Eye guess its easy to say that Eye overlooked a lot of things because the things my heart felt for Candace. Candace's mother felt comfortable with me because when she couldn't reach Candace, she'd call my phone. Candace phone was either dead because she loved making videos on her Youtbe channel or had it on vibrate where she couldn't hear it.

> *"How well do you know the person you're with {spouse, mate, companion, significant other, lover, etc.}? Would they ever betray you? Would/ Could they be there or by your side if you really needed them? Would/ Could they vouch for your character in a positive way?*
>
> *Would they be willing to give up a kidney or blood if you were a match and needed them? Could it be you thought you KNEW them, only to realize that you've been "Sleeping with the enemy" the entire time?*
>
> *POINT: Circumstances/ situations alter people's perceptions, interpretations and lives daily. The person you're giving the "Mantle of Trust" to, could be the very one that has a motive to destroy you!" – Lamont Bershawn.*

When Eye flew home this time there was a bit of tension because things were being revealed that started making me ask myself questions. Candace began showing me a different, much more classier side of her. She started showing me that she too wanted this relationship more than ever. She already had a number of videos on social media that was showing her fanbase the loving, caring and giving man Eye am. To add to it a few days after Eye left, Candace received

EYE'VE STOOD INSIDE THE EYE OF HELL AND REMAINED FEARLESS!

paperwork from Tyrone's attorney stating that he's withdrawing from the case and no further action is permitted. The Judge also gave her paperwork granting her divorce. All of this was great news to me and was more important than what was revealed to me, although Eye didn't forget them.

Eye never discussed anything with my family because Eye didn't want them to judge her according to the things Eye was feeling. Eye could tell Candace was carrying a bunch of issues within because she'd always repeat certain things as if she wasn't ever good enough. Candace kept saying, "I apologize, I'm sorry, I won't do it again, Am I enough for you, it was the church or my mother never taught us." Eye hugged Candace and asked her, "what's bothering you?" She just cried and said, "I just don't want to mess up." We began talking about her marriages in detail because Eye wanted to get to the bottom of whatever it was traumatizing her. Candace told me in her first marriage her husband punched her in the head and her third marriage he bit her in the face amongst other psychological and physical abuse. Eye remember Candace pulling up a Youtube video and her last ex- husband Tyrone made the statement, "you're not going to be good for anyone because I'm going to make sure you're psychologically fucked up." Then it dawned on me, Tyrone and Candace role played a lot and put their lives out in social media. Whether he played a pimp and she played the prostitute or she played the drug user and he, the drug dealer. My interest isn't in social media, but it was making Candace my wife. Eye realized it was hard for her to cut social media loose because that's where she received validation, attention and life.

Candace called me after work on a Thursday and said that she was going to the casino with the few extra dollars she had. When she returned home from the casino she called me. Eye asked, "how did you do?" Candace responded, "I could kick my own ass. I gambled my entire check and now I don't have the money to pay my bills." Eye began to sit back and close my eyes, "what do you mean you gambled your entire check?" Eye believe Candace felt that Eye had a soft spot for her crying because that's what she started doing. She began to hyperventilate over the phone and Eye had to tell her to calm down and breathe. Eye asked her, "how much money do you need?" Candace replied, "eight hundred dollars." Without hesitation Eye said, "Eye'm going to let you borrow eight hundred dollars because this is all your fault, otherwise Eye would have given it to you." Candace agreed. She was relieved and Eye sent it through cash app. Again, Candace began bragging about the type of man she has on social media. The same few that was commenting on her posts and videos were the same ones interested in getting the same treatment from me. One thing about me, when Eye dedicate myself to something or someone Eye'm totally committed. Candace wasn't used to a loyal man. Eye was so committed and loyal to Candace that Eye created the word, LOVALTY.

> *There's plenty of people that think loving someone is enough in a relationship, but is it?*
> *Absolutely not!*
> *Have you ever loved someone but still had reservations of doing things for them, helping them financially or spending quality time with them?*
> *Have you ever loved someone but found it easier to be intimate with someone else?*
> *Eye don't want anyone to get upset or mad but many religious people believe their god of choice is love.*
> *Which brings up a challenging question, "Does love hurt, heal or is it neutral?"*
> *Allow me to introduce to you a word that most of you will begin to honor in your relationship or marriage. The word is "Lovalty!"*
> *Lovalty is love + loyalty. It gives you the power to reject anything/ anyone that is engaged to dishonor your word or vow to another.*
> *Lovalty begins with honoring and respecting SELF! – Lamont Bershawn.*

EYE'VE STOOD INSIDE THE EYE OF HELL AND REMAINED FEARLESS!

It was almost time for me to fly back out to visit Candace over the Halloween weekend. Eye went to the bank and withdrew three thousand dollars for the purpose of helping her with her bills and doing something fun and productive. This visit Candace and Eye went to the movies, the mall, lotta burger and then she wanted to go to the casino. Once again, Candace didn't have any money so Eye told her to pick out a machine and we'd tag team it, just to see how she responded to doing something together. She didn't accept that too well which led me to believe people took things from her or she was just a selfish person. Eye initially put three hundred dollars in the machine just to see what it would do and Candace made each bet. Eye won five hundred dollars and cashed out the ticket. Candace didn't want to cash out but let it accrue. Eye explained to her that it's a gamble, but Eye refuse to lose when Eye'm a few hundred ahead. Eye won an additional six hundred, cashed out and split it with Candace. Now she has three hundred dollars to do whatever she pleased. What did she do? Lost it all. Meanwhile, Eye'm on the other end of the casino winning. Eye won a total of two thousand dollars by cashing out every $500.00 win. It was still early so Candace had to make a stop to the loan company she borrowed money from. Eye asked her, "how much did she need to pay the loan off?" "Candace said, $400.00." This solidified what Eye was feeling, "Candace was extremely bad with finances." Candace asked to borrow another $500.00 and she'd pay me from her next pay. Eye agreed and let her borrow the money.

"When a man loves a woman. He clings to the fiber of her very being. He understands her heart and gets to know her heartbeat in essence to become one with her, instead of trying to possess or control her.

He puts forth every effort to make sure she's protected, "Covered" physically, mentally, financially and emotionally.

There's NOT a thing he would resist doing because he KNOWS that she's the {Wisdom} that propels his every move and desire. When a

LAMONT BERSHAWN

man loves a woman, he's willing to give up his SELFish ego! – Lamont Bershawn.

Eye thought she was going to pay off her loan, but instead she took all of it to the casino in hopes of hitting a jackpot. Eye didn't have an issue with going to the casino my issue was not being able to leave when you're ahead $300.00. Candace had a problem leaving with her winnings. No wonder she was comfortable with her living arrangements, everything she'd earn would either go to the casino or a fashion statement. Candace had a good heart but was a very troubled person. Eye think Eye aided in being partly therapeutic for her because Eye did things for her that no one had ever done in a relationship. Prior to me leaving this time Eye paid for her flight for Thanksgiving and for her birthday in mid- December to visit me.

When Eye got home, Eye began getting things prepared for our wedding day. Eye got on the laptop and called Candace on the phone to see exactly what we needed and where our honeymoon would take place. Candace said she wanted to go to Las Vegas. Eye called to book flights and make reservations for Las Vegas when the call was interrupted by my favorite cousin Nancy. Nancy asked me, "what was I doing?" "Eye'm about to make reservations for my honeymoon." "Where are you going?" "Candace wants to go to Las Vegas." Nancy says, "Don't pay for it. My husband and I are giving you use of our villa for your honeymoon, all you have to do is purchase your flights." Eye was in awe and thankful. Eye had to invite them along with my mother on the honeymoon. Eye asked, "Candace to ask her mother if she'd like to come, but she said, "no." Eye immediately purchased everyone's flight to Las Vegas for our honeymoon. Candace wanted a very lavish wedding but didn't have the money to fulfill her desires. Eye explained to Candace that my main objective is to have a very nice wedding and reception and living a decent life after all is said and done. Candace became irate and said, "I don't want a junk wedding or a pieced together wedding." Eye responded, "Have Eye ever done anything half assed to you, with you or for you? Please understand that my taste is impeccable and you should know that Eye'm not cheap." Eye made another agreement with Candace since she wanted a lavish wedding. Candace agreed to pay half of every dime Eye spent buying the things she wanted for the wedding, minus the honeymoon, photographer and disc jockey {those were my expenses}. We talked about how money was going to be disbursed after the wedding. Out of the blue Candace said, "none of my family will be giving any gifts. Their gift to me will be showing up for the occasion." Eye responded, "that's not a gift Candace. You mean to tell me that none of your family will give you a card with money or a toaster?" My heart quickly became sad as Eye remembered a few conversations we had. Eye can very well see why Candace's heart was hardened at times.

> *"Family members that constantly say, "I love you" yet desire to pacify or cover up the truth with lies just to appease you don't love you. They're causing you more harm than helping because they're not allowing you to deal with your internalized pain." – Lamont Bershawn.*

It seemed that Candace had to grow up fast because her father was an alcoholic doing his own thing and her mother wasn't paying much attention to her neither. This is why Candace was sheltered in the church in order to keep her out of trouble and harm's way. Eye spoke with Candace's sister Lois and she said, "Candace is my heart. She's been through so much in her life from childhood up until this very moment. Lamont, I'm glad you're with her. You have to be gentle with her because she's very fragile." Eye responded, "Eye'll never hit her and Eye'm doing everything that Eye can to show her that Eye'm nothing like those men she's used to dealing with. When Eye was visiting her and she felt that Eye was going to leave her, Candace began hyperventilating like she was about to have an asthma attack."

Eye spent approximately $3000.00 ordering chair covers, lights, linen table cloths, chair sashes, plates, silverware, chrome trimmed glasses, favors, invitations, etc. On top of all of that Eye bought her grandchildren's dresses because two of them were going to be flower girl's. Everything was coming together as planned, just a few minor scratches during the process.

Candace flew to visit me during the Thanksgiving holiday's and my mother made a beautiful spread. Candace made a "dump cake" which is a quick dessert that consisted of pouring fruit inside of a pan, then pouring golden cake mix on top of that and covering entire pan with margarine. When completed that process, bake for 25 minutes at 350 degrees. Eye learned that Candace either didn't want to cook, didn't like to cook or only could cook a few things well. Candace could fry corn using a half a pound of butter, frito chili pie, eggs and cream of wheat. She didn't know what hominy grits were but she liked them after Eye made her some. After we ate Thanksgiving dinner we went to the casino to gamble for a few hours. Eye gave my mother a few hundred dollars and Eye gave Candace a couple hundred to play. When Candace was out of money, she came and sat next to me, watching for a moment and then wanted to get cuddly like a kitten walking on a person's lap. Eye knew she wanted to borrow more money but Eye kept playing. Once again, Eye let her borrow $300.00 and she hit $2200.00. Eye knew she had obligations at home so Eye didn't ask for any money, but she paid me $200.00 of the $1100.00 she owed me. Eye wasn't pressed for the money being as though she was going to be my wife, meaning what belongs to me is also hers.

> *"Some people have a beautiful look on the exterior but have a spirit that's totally contrary. In other word's NEVER judge a person or a book by its covering because when you decide to explore the pages or get to know what's beyond the cover, you'll begin to see it's nothing but Damaged Goods!" – Lamont Bershawn.*

Candace had to leave the next afternoon to head back home, but she knew she'd be back in a few weeks for her birthday. We laughed, joked around with each other and enjoyed cuddling and watching television, well as long as she could stay awake. Eye knew Candace felt safe in my arms because Eye never did anything to hurt or harm her. Eye told her, "Eye'd never hurt, harm nor hinder you. Eye don't care who did what to you in your past, always remember that Eye'm not them." Candace said, "Thank you! You're nothing like anyone I ever dealt with and this experience I'm sharing with you has never happened. No one has ever cared for me as deep as you're expressing to me. Thank you, Lamont." "Candace, Eye'll never disrespect, dishonor, degrade, devalue or destroy what we're building together", was the only thing Eye wanted her to always remember.

Candace flew back home and the first time she didn't feel the need to buy a drink prior to boarding the airplane. Eye felt things were finally taking shape to get us more on a direct path for each other. When she settled down after arriving home, she video chatted with me and we had a heart to heart conversation of the things we were feeling up to this point in our relationship. Eye wanted us to have a clean slate with each other which meant any issues or problems we harbored with each other or anyone else, get them out of our system. Eye started off by telling Candace that Eye didn't like her spending habits that forced me to continue bailing her out. Eye suggested to her that instead of always going to the casino because Eye realized it was an outlet of hers, not so much that she enjoyed it, to take whatever excess money and get the important things out of the pawn shop. Candace was surviving by pawning her car title, electric appliances, computer and television getting deeper in debt. The casino was just a chance that she'd take to get extra money. Candace began seeing things differently. The only thing Candace was concerned with was that Eye'd make her dress like a church missionary. Eye explained to Candace, "Eye haven't been in church in a long time and Eye'm not about to make her dress like a missionary. Eye explained to Candace that she can look classy and sexy without revealing her augmented parts to the world. Again, we had an understanding. Candace had a few hundred dollars that seemed to be burning her pocket, so she said, "I'm feeling lucky tonight, so I'm going to press my luck at the casino." Eye said, "Good luck. Eye hope you win big." She called me from the car as she was driving to the casino and video chatted briefly as she was walking inside the casino. Thirty minutes later Eye receive a call from Candace saying, "I just hit a jackpot for $13,000.00." Eye was elated because now she could pay me the $4500.00 she owed me. Yes, between borrowing and me bailing her out that's what it came up to. She did what was right with the money by paying her bills, getting her belongings from the pawn shop that she borrowed money on and giving her mother a few dollars. At the end of paying everything and everyone she owed, Candace was left with $300.00. She didn't like it, but Eye reminded her that financially she had a clean slate and wasn't behind anymore. The entire week went fine without any issues and we still were sleeping with each other via video chat. Deep down on the inside Eye felt that she didn't trust me because she wasn't being honest and true to me or to herself.

> *"No guilt is forgotten so long as the conscience still knows of it!"* – Stefan Zweig

The day prior to catching the flight to me we were video chatting and she asked if she could borrow so money to get her nails done and money to pay for her baggage fees for her flight? She added, "I never went a birthday or any holiday without having them done." Eye told Candace, "If that was the case then you'd have them done because you knew you were coming up. Your nails is not a priority of mine. Ever since we've been together Eye've taken care of my responsibilities and part yours too. You're going to have to start doing better or we're not going to make it together. Eye'm not the fall guy." In the end, Eye cash app her the money needed. No matter how frustrated Eye may have gotten, Eye always seemed to give in. Eye did everything because Eye loved her beyond my actions or words could express, but Eye didn't lose myself in the relationship.

Candace was off for an entire week. Two days after Candace arrived we drove up to the mountains because Monday was opening season for buck {male deer}. We packed our bags and she had the chance to try on the fluorescent orange outfit required to be in the woods. Candace wasn't going to hunt, she was there to experience something new. The moment we were about to leave the house to head to the hotel Candace began crying. Eye asked her, "why are you crying, what's wrong?" Candace replied, "I'm scared." "What are you afraid of Candace? Do you think I'm going to let anything happen to you?" Candace said, "I don't want to be shot by the white people?" "If it's any consolation we don't have to go this time. I'll just wait until next week and go during doe {female deer} season. White people are hunting too and Eye'm going to have a rifle and gun as most will, so there's nothing to be afraid of. You're going to be directly by my side." Candace agreed to go and we were on our way. Candace recorded and enjoyed seeing the snow on top of the mountains and the beautiful scenery while headed to the mountains. We get to the hotel, watch the football game, made passionate love and fell asleep. We were a little hungry when we awakened, so we went to grab a bite and came back in to get showered up for the morning.

The next morning was finally here and we're up at five o'clock a.m. preparing to drive to the woods to go hunting. As we approached the state game lands there were plenty of cars parked at the bottom of the hill near the wide opened field. Off a distance as Eye slowed down driving up the hill a ten point {number of antler points on his head} buck was running from one end of the field, but it was too early to shoot, besides he was near someone's farm. When we parked in the parking area we loaded up and prepared to go into the woods. Candace carried the flashlight while Eye had my rifle and a firearm on my hip. Eye knew the area so we walked in and Eye cleaned off an area where we both sat within arms reach apart. We sat for a few hours and saw a glimpse of a tail but Eye didn't have a clear shot. We took a break for lunch and walked to the vehicle. It wasn't a lot of hunters where we were so nothing was really moving. As we sat in the vehicle I was about to drive to the top of the mountain, but too many cars were up there so Eye turned around, parked and we headed to our same exact location. Eye loved this location and spot because Eye've killed several deer from it and Eye thought it would be a great opportunity for Candace to see some action. Candace began looking on social media, browsing through Facebook when, we heard a sound coming about 30 paces above Candace, it was another hunter. He saw us and Candace moved to the tree to my left, while the other hunter walked around us on the high end. That's when Eye heard a quicker trot from below and when Eye looked up there were two bucks trotting about fifty meters away. Eye scoped the head to see if they were legal to shoot. They dashed away and separated from each other. Eye took a shot from the seated position, one from kneeling position and the fatal shot came from when Eye stood up. Candace began recording from the very first shot Eye fired. Eye looked back at Candace and said, "got him." We walked down the hill, across the path and there the eight- point buck was laying dead. Candace was excited and then asked, "how are we going to get this big mutha fukka to the vehicle?" Eye said, "once Eye gut him, he'll be lighter enough for me to drag to the truck." It took me thirty minutes to drag him to the truck but Candace did help toss him into the back of the truck. When we left the area, as Eye drove down the hill back to the hotel we saw plenty of hunters and deer running in the fields but not too many shots being fired. Eye was extremely glad that we weren't going back empty handed and most of all Candace's first hunting experience produced results. It was the moment of a lifetime for me because Eye felt Candace and Eye were supposed to be together forever and this moment guaranteed it, because she was here with me when Eye killed the deer.

Attachment vs. Connection:

Please understand there's a difference between being attached to something/ someone opposed to being connected.

Being attached does NOT mean there's a connection.

An attachment consists of something/ someone that's DEPENDENT upon the other.
Example:

(1) {a leech/ parasite feeding off a living organism for survival}
(2) {One sided relationship}
(3) {a hook & cable towing a car}

EYE'VE STOOD INSIDE THE EYE OF HELL AND REMAINED FEARLESS!

A connection is a collective, equal partisan, dual shared union/meeting on common ground. In other words, of the same mindset. Two individual parallels coming together forming one powerful unit.
Example:

(1) {an electrical light switch}
(2) {two people coming together creating an intimate port}
(3) {causal or logical relation or sequence}

Some of you are in a relationship and you're wondering why you're still there

(1) *wondering why things aren't working out*
(2) *wondering why you're not getting the attention that you feel you deserve*
(3) *wondering who the hell is this person... because it's certainly NOT the individual you gave access to your heart.*

Well, have you ever thought or considered that you're ONLY attached to the person and there's no REAL CONNECTION?
POINT: Recognizing your connection is more valuable than misunderstanding/ misinterpreting your attachment to anything/ anyone!! – Lamont Bershawn.

Eye was beginning to feel that Candace was more attached to me opposed to being connected, although she kept telling me, "you're the air I breathe." Why was Eye feeling this way about the woman Eye asked to marry me? What was bringing these things to my mind? These thoughts began to come across my mind heavily, but Eye trusted the things she said to me.

When we arrived back to the house, we unpacked and headed shopping. Eye took Candace shopping for intimate apparel {panties, bras, etc.}. She picked out clothes that fit and not tight. She finally had bras that was her correct size and she felt great about them. On our way back home, Eye bought her a birthday cake, took her out to dinner and of course on top of that Eye gave her money to gamble while being at the casino. Candace said, "this was by far the best birthday I'd ever experienced." Eye ordered her Christmas gift a few days later although Eye knew we wouldn't spend Christmas together because she had more days off for the New Year. Enjoying every moment, we were spending together and not taking it for granted, Eye decided to ask Candace when did she plan on relocating up here with me? We decided that the middle of February would be great timing for her to adjust and settle in. We didn't stay long at the casino because we had a long and busy day, so we went to the hotel, cuddled and held each other the rest of the night.

The next morning, Eye cooked breakfast for her and we watched rerun's of "Power" before Eye had to drop her off at the airport.

Candace made it home safely and realized that her internet service was interrupted. When Candace called me on video chat she said, "My internet service was cut off and I don't have the money to pay the bill. Can you pay it for me and I'll reimburse you on my next check?" Eye asked Candace, "How much is the bill?" The bill was $350.00 because she never paid the bill in full, she'd pay the minimum to keep the service on which meant every month coming up the balance would increase from what was past due. because she didn't pay the bill. Candace's mother and sister didn't have the money to get it turned back on, her daughter didn't have the money and her son refused to help her pay her bill. Candace asked me, "how much did you pay for my ring?" Eye thought that was odd for her to ask. Eye started thinking that she had intentions on pawning the ring to get money to pay off a few of her bills and then tell me a lie. Eye mean the ring is insured. Deep down on the inside Eye knew that Candace hated to call and ask me to borrow the money. The first thing that crossed my mind was, "what is she doing with her money?" Eye paid her bill in full to prevent her from going into the office because she was working from home. "Thank you so much Lamont because I really didn't want to go into the office", Candace responded. Eye recognized that something deeper was going on with Candace finances because she'd get paid from her job and win sometimes at the casino but she never had any money. Was she spending it on drugs or liquor? Was she just telling me a lie so that she could build up her finances as long as Eye'd give or was she taking my money and giving spending it on someone else? Was Candace playing me for a fool? Candace was "bridge paying" {paying the necessary portion to keep things functioning} all of her bills. When Eye went to sleep those thoughts weighed heavy on my mind and if Eye didn't address it eventually things would come to the surface or brought into the light.

Is your spouse, companion, significant other or mate more of a weight than a help?

MARRIED FOLK:

"Until death do we part." **DOES NOT** *mean for you to remain in a marriage until either of you transition from this earth. There's some people who are experiencing (1) mental abuse (2) emotional abuse (3) are being disrespected on every level (4) physical abuse {NOT including dominatrix if that's what you're into}, etc.*

Many times, a person will experience a "Spiritual death/ Spiritual Disconnection" and a "Physical Dismembering" prior to the "Physical death." The spiritual death is totally connected to your spirit, which are inner feelings/ emotions. These feelings are TRUE and are NOT to be discounted, overlooked or set aside.

Here's a few examples of a "Spiritual death": (1) When you're feeling lonely/ alone in the presence of your spouse. Isolation (2) When you no longer can stand being intimate with your spouse (3) When you become numb to anything your spouse says (4) When you find yourself taking long hours to even come home to be in the company of your spouse, etc.

If you've gotten to the point in your marriage that you're no longer living/ loving and maintaining a healthy attitude then it's imperative to make a few changes. You've become physically drained, spiritually impaired and religiously indoctrinated to the point that you don't know which way to turn. The time is NOW to release ALL weights, burdens and hindrances. Stop waiting for an outside force to intervene!!

SINGLE but ATTACHED with NO ties {children, real estate, etc.} whatsoever:

If not "married" and have no ties whatsoever, why are you still in it?

Is it because of the sex? (2) the fear of leaving and learning another person? (3) stability?

If you're still involved in a partnership/ relationship and are miserable without any ties, then you're the weight and therefore have a motive/ agenda the reason you're waiting.

SINGLE with ties:

"If you're happy and you know it, clap your hands!!"

If you're miserable and wish that you've never met the individual, well it's a bit too late for that. The time now is to either turn the "lemons into lemonade" or find the area that both will benefit all parties and remain respectful but cordial.

Eye know deep down on the inside you've asked, "Who the fuck is this person?" Eye made a mistake because certainly this isn't the same individual Eye gave access to my heart.

Don't worry, it's not the end of the world... lol.

{This category must be another separate post...lol}. Meanwhile make the best of your situation}!!

Whether "married" or "single", you'll never stop meeting people {sexually, networking, friendships, etc.}. Try their spirit by the spirit living within. If there's static or if your spirit repel/ rebel then don't force something that's not there. Most people get caught up early making a seasonal person a lifetime commitment!! – Lamont Bershawn.

Too many questions started to arise and too many red flags were standing erect awaiting to be cut down. Eye decided no matter the cost, Eye'd make reservations to spend Christmas with Candace and book the ticket on my return so that we'll end up flying together. Once again, Eye'm being relentless in my effort to keep the flames burning in our relationship. Eye arrived on Christmas and we shared our first Christmas together. We didn't exchange gifts because Eye left her gift at my house. The quality time was more important to me because Eye wasn't going to allow anything to hinder our relationship. Eye remember briefly stopping by her mother's house to make a plate of food to go. Eye had free nights at the casino and we decided to take advantage of the offer. Two days before New Years Day, we took our first flight together. When we boarded the aircraft, Candace took our picture and a selfie, but posted her selfie as if the photo we took together wasn't important or good enough to post on social media. It was as if she wasn't engaged to be married and all alone and

Eye no longer mattered. Candace faithfully wore the ring though. We slept on both flights and when we landed we took the shuttle to my car which was parked at the airport lot. We usually would go to the casino but instead we went straight to the hotel where we had a minor issue with management. We finally entered our room after waiting for someone at the front desk for an hour and got settled in.

The next morning, we went to my mother's house where wedding supplies were coming in that Eye ordered. Candace was shocked to see all of the bouquets made the flower girls baskets and the pillow for the ring bearer. Eye walked upstairs and grabbed one of Candace's Christmas gifts and gave it to her. It was a video camera for her car in case of an accident or being stopped by the police, everything would be recorded. Candace didn't buy me a gift but it didn't matter because my gift was spending the New Year with my mother and Candace. The casino gave me a free night at the hotel along with dinner for two because Eye'm considered a "high roller" so Candace and Eye took advantage of the perks. The room was very nice and the food was delicious. We stayed at the casino long enough to see the ball drop at times square on the television and the we went back to the hotel before people started drinking and driving. When we arrived back at the hotel we took a shower together and then Eye gave Candace her other gift. It was a red lace negligee where her tits were totally free. She loved it and wore it well. The love making was intense to the point Candace had to stop because Eye was pole driving the walls of her pussy that she finished it out by sucking my dick and swallowing my cum. Don't get me wrong, Eye totally gave respect to the pussy but it was the very first day of a New Year.

> *Pussy: "Sweet enough to bring you into existence; yet deadly enough to take you out of existence!!"*
>
> *RESPECT: In my life or Eye should say, "Respectfully", through my experience{s}. Eye've learned to Honor, Respect, Love, Cherish, Pass up, but NEVER get "Caught up" with falling in love with the vagina.*

EYE'VE STOOD INSIDE THE EYE OF HELL AND REMAINED FEARLESS!

> *What Eye've learned is that it feels as cushiony as a pillow of cotton; it tastes like cotton candy; and it smells like fresh chamomile - RESPECT!*
>
> *It has the power to give birth to an entire universe yet has the power to bring an army of soldiers to their knees - RESPECT!*
>
> *Yes, Eye've learned to respect the power of love {Stephanie Mills}; but Eye've also learned to respect the "Nectar" that gives life and also has the power to take life/freedom - RESPECT!!*
>
> *{Dedicated to those brothers who refused to believe and accept the power of the vagina. To the brothers we've lost to it, the brothers who killed for it, got killed by it or lost their freedom because of it - RESPECT!!}!! - Lamont Bershawn.*

All we wanted to do the next day was rest. We awakened later in the afternoon and went to my mother's because Jerome and his fiancée was in town. Mom cooked dinner and we ate and the watched a movie. Everyone stayed at mom's that night so she wouldn't be alone. Jerome and Eye couldn't see Eye to Eye on a lot of things and Eye just couldn't trust him based on his track record with me, but somehow Eye found myself doing anything to please my mother.

"Love Lifted ME!!"

> *Eye've learned to accept the good, bad and indifferent in others. Knowing that Eye refuse to allow the "Enemy" to connect to my "Inner-Me" in order to take my focus off my very own path.*
>
> *Eye refuse to denounce an ounce of my energy because it's all about my "Inner G" that's keeping me in tuned with my reality.*

Eye've realized that we're all cut from the same cloth, yet we wear different fabric. The fragrance of innocence that came from the birthright of LOVE being dragged through the muddy waters that was sent from above?

The heavens that Eye thought Eye had to look up and pray to in order to hear my Gods voice could never give me an answer. Why?

It was the heaven that resided in my mind, my consciousness, my thought, my internal compass; that would keep me from the eternal burning hell that was a scare tactic that plagued my mind as a child.

Eye had to stop listening to everything and everyone on the exterior of my being. Many voices that Eye thought loved and cared about me because they were simply those Eye called family.

Running back and forth to the church seeking an answer, a word or a sign. Little did Eye know it was the place where the lost would always dine.

Somehow, Eye knew that Eye would never find "Thee", until Eye realized that the "Thee" Eye was in search of was the LOVE that lived within ME!! – Lamont Bershawn.

Here we are the beginning of a new year that we celebrated together as an engaged couple. Eye felt in my heart that things started right and they'd end up right, Eye mean what could possibly go wrong? We had three full months before our wedding day. Candace made it back home and was making preparations to move up here permanently. At first, Candace suggested that Eye rent a truck down there and pack her belongings in it and we drive the 19 hours. That was a great idea until Eye realized everything was all on me. Eye asked Candace, "what are you planning on bringing?" Candace replied,

EYE'VE STOOD INSIDE THE EYE OF HELL AND REMAINED FEARLESS!

"my shoes, clothes, work computers and my good wigs. All of it can actually fit inside my car." Eye responded, "Okay, but if not, we'll rent a truck and get a dolly to tow your vehicle." Eye went on the computer to check prices for a truck rental and received an email from Hard Rock Casino that Criss Angel was going to be there for a one- night performance. This is one of the attractions that Eye wanted us to see during our honeymoon, but he wasn't scheduled to perform. Eye immediately told Candace, "Eye'm going to purchase tickets to see Criss Angel perform the end of January, would you like to go?" Candace had no idea who Criss Angel {one of the greatest illusionist's} is. Eye began looking at the calendar and asked Candace, "would you like to relocate with me sooner than we discussed? Eye was thinking that Eye could purchase a one- way flight there and we can drive your car back together. It would be easier on the both of us." Candace agreed and now we had to make the necessary adjustments for two weeks instead of one month.

The time had come for me to fly out to Candace. This time Eye wouldn't have to leave her side, she wouldn't have to worry about dropping me off at the airport and we didn't have to be sad any longer about departing from one another. Eye booked a room at the casino so we'd be right there for the show and didn't have to drive. The Criss Angel show was amazing as expected. Eye bought us each a Criss Angel shirt as a souvenir to remember our first show together. The next morning, Candace was excited because her check hit her account. Eye said, "yay, we have a little bit of gambling money." Candace looked at me and said harshly with a sarcastic attitude, "you aint getting none of this money." A few hours later, we went downstairs to gamble a little. Candace withdrew $300.00 and asked me, "where are you going to play?" "Eye replied, "on the other side." Candace said, "good luck" and walked away. Eye had money but Eye was no longer interested in gambling, so Eye bought a snack from the gift shop and headed back to the room. Candace called my cell phone an hour later and asked, "where are you?" Eye responded, "in the room." Moments later, Candace entered the room. Eye was sitting on the bed watching the football game. Candace looked at me and the expression Eye had on my face was a dead giveaway that something was on my mind. Candace asked, "what's wrong?" Eye responded, "Eye felt some sort of way when you said in a harsh sarcastic tone, "YOU AINT GETTING NONE OF THIS MONEY" when all Eye've ever done was GIVE, GIVE, GIVE without any hesitation or reservation. Eye never thought Eye'd say this but, "maybe you're not the one for me!" In an instant, Candace pulled a few winning tickets out of her pocket and said, "I was only joking around." Eye looked at her and said, "no you weren't. If you were joking you would have made the offer when you withdrew your money." Candace sat on the foot of the bed and started to cry, saying, "I'm sorry!" Eye forgave Candace but Eye could tell that the men she dealt with never freely gave her anything. Eye kept showing her and telling Candace, "Eye'm not like the men you're used to dealing with." Candace replied, "I know you're not. I dealt with people who took advantage of me and my kindness for many years. I never had a real man like you in my life. No one ever wanted to share anything positive with me. Now, you enter my life at 56 and I'm not used to this. I'm trying though. I need you to know that I love you, I need you and you've become the air I breathe, my all in all, my soulmate. Eye began replaying and rewinding things we previously dealt with and said to myself, "either Candace is playing the role to get her Oscar, she's really being sincere or she's full of shit." Eye took her as being apologetic and sincere. Eye thought, maybe the move will give her a better sense of who Eye really am and that Eye truly wanted to make her my wife because Eye genuinely loved and cared for her well-being. There wasn't anything Eye wouldn't do for Candace.

Two days later, Candace's mother had to go to the hospital because her equilibrium was off which caused her to lose her balance. Candace's sister, Monica called Candace to give her the news. Candace called her job and took the rest of the day off, as Eye would, which was approved by her boss. Candace's boss already approved the following Tuesday to Friday for travel purposes, so technically once she got off work Candace's vacation started. Candace and Eye met up with Monica to see how their mother was doing. Candace's older sister, Amy was already there. When we walked into her mother's room to see how she was doing, she was eating food that the hospital provided, but she had the strength to talk. Candace told her mother, "we're leaving at some point today to hit the road. I love you mom." Candace's mother held Candace's hand and said, "I know you two can make it together. I can tell that Lamont loves you and I feel so good about him. You know when you were getting married before I had my reservations, but I allowed you to make your own choice. Remember you have to be there for each other and not be selfish. A marriage can't grow if either of you aren't willing to listen and be there for one another. I'm not going to hold you so you all have a safe trip. Thank you, Lamont, for loving and being so wonderful to my daughter." Just the things Candace's mother said let me know that Eye did my very best to make things work. If nothing else, Eye had her mother's approval. While sitting in the hospital bed eating Candace's mother looked at her and said, "You work for the insurance company and can put Lamont on your insurance, which will be beneficial for both of you." Candace replied, "Lamont already has insurance." Well, Eye do but we never discussed any of that. Once again, my mind started throwing up red flags. "Does Candace really have my best interest at heart or is she just thinking about herself?" "Am Eye making one of the biggest mistakes of my life?" When we got in the car Eye told Candace, "we don't have to leave today because Eye wouldn't want things to get worse while we were traveling and had to turn around. If it were my mother, Eye'd wait a day or two." Candace was adamant about leaving and relocating.

RESPECT THE VOICE:

Why is "God" only choosing who to speak to, bless, prophesy through or use as a testimony? So many people think that "God" only speaks within the confines of a church, but that's TOTALLY FALSE.

There's those people who profess their belief in "God" but refuse to step outside of their set denominations/ religions {A.M.E, Baptist, Pentecostal, C.M.E, Holiness, Gods only,

Christlike, Catholic, Methodist, Episcopal, Mormon, C.O.G.I.C, etc.}

The church leaders have caused many to remain ignorant, enslaved, selfless and dependent upon the church for many solutions that there's no answer that the church can conceivably answer. Many people have conformed to the "Sacred" books for answers because of (1) negative situations/ circumstances (2) life's experiences (3) relationship/ marital problems (4) financial help (5) family concerns, etc.

Let's see if we've ever REALLY recognized the "VOICE!":

The "Voice" has many names {intuition, instinct, consciousness/ conscience, "God" within, Chi, inner man, power that be, etc.}.

(1) Have you ever been somewhere and the "Voice" spoke with you telling you to "Get the hell out of this place NOW?" {you listened only to find out something bad happened moments after your departure!!}

(2) Have you ever been driving and the "Voice" took you on another route, contrary to your normal way of travel? {later to find out you avoided a fatal accident!!}

(3) Have you ever ignored the "Voice" and found yourself in trouble? {happens daily with people}

(4) Have you missed out on a "Blessing" by following someone else's path instead of listening to the "Voice?" {of course}

(5) Have you and your friend ever been at a location and the "Voice" told you to "Immediately leave these premises?" Your friend looked at your expression and

dropped everything to follow you!! {Your friend tells you I saw a look in your eye that ALERTED me. That was the power of discernment within your friend to recognize the power within you. Later to find out, the location you left was robbed and bombed.}

{The above are examples of coincidences that may have been a similarity in your life}
The "VOICE" is YOUR PERSONAL "SPIRITUAL GOD/ FORCE" that directs/ guides YOU!! The reason NOBODY else can hear the "Voice" that YOU hear is because it's designed distinctively for YOU. It's there to protect/ guide you so RECOGNIZE IT, RESPECT IT and REACT/ RESPOND TO IT!!

There's a number of reasons why your prayers have NOT been answered. Eye believe many have missed the "Voice of God" because YOU were listening for the "Deep" voice of a man. Who's to say it's NOT the soft, subtle and nurturing voice of a woman {Wisdom}?

No wonder there's so many who are considered "Lost." They've been misled by the "Wrong" voice and refused to "Hear" the voice that was constantly trying to connect with their spirit.

POINT: There's a "Feminine" being/ attribute in all aspects of creation {humans, animals, insects, etc.}. Don't ever disregard the woman because it's her that all creation came into existence through. The "VOICE" is compatible to that which "gender" YOU can comprehend from or receive better information. In {Re-LIE-Gion} men are placed upon pedestals *as the "High Priest." Let "Them" who have an ear to hear pay close attention to what "She" has to say. She speaks VOLUMES!! – Lamont Bershawn.*

    Eye disregarded my very own advice, most assuredly because everything was already packed inside of the car. Once we left the hospital we were going to begin our nineteen- hour journey together. That's another reason Eye didn't cancel the trip because Eye felt the long drive would give us time to discuss whatever was on our minds. Candace just got paid, so Eye knew she had a few dollars to contribute towards this trip. Eye filled up the car and she started driving until she got tired. Candace drove until it was time to fill up again. When she pulled up to the gas station Eye said, "we'll split the finances for the trip", just to hear what her response would be. Candace responded, "Eye didn't think Eye had to help or contribute for the trip." If we were close to a major airport, Eye would have taken over and drove directly there and caught a flight home. Candace wasn't a "team player", she wanted a Queen lifestyle being a beggar, pauper or by the hard work of another. In other words, she always had an excuse when it came to contributing to anything.

    While we were at the gas station we used the restroom and picked up a few snacks for the long trip. Eye stopped at a fast food restaurant to grab us some food further into the trip. Approximately nine hours into the trip Eye hit a hole in the road that gave us a flat. Eye wasn't worried because a week prior to flying out to get Candace Eye asked her to make sure she had a spare tire and her fluids were changed on her vehicle. Well, Eye was on the phone with her when she was getting the oil changed because she didn't know whether to use conventional oil or synthetic. Eye told her to get synthetic to be safe. When Eye pulled over to a safe place, Eye pulled everything out of the trunk and the spare tire was old, dry rotten and it didn't even fit the car. In other words, Candace never checked her spare tire. It seemed that Candace was making things hard for me and Eye knew that Eye wouldn't be able to adjust. Eye called AAA {American Automobile Association} became a member since she didn't have roadside assistance on her car. Eye was puzzled that she had so many life insurance policies on people but wasn't a member of AAA since her son worked for them. We were safely parked in the parking lot under plenty of light. We waited six hours for AAA and they towed us to Walmart where Eye paid for a new tire. Eye didn't get any rest because Eye was a little frustrated, but we seemed to turn that moment into a laughing matter. Eye continued to drive and Eye stopped to get us some breakfast. We were "smooth sailing" while Candace slept peacefully Eye was driving, listening to music, singing and thinking at the same time. When Candace woke up we were about an hour away from my house. Eye filled up the car again and we decided to grab something to eat from the restaurant before hitting the road again. Eye asked Candace is she okay to start driving? She said, "yes."

When we arrived to the house, we immediately began taking things out of the car and putting them where they belonged. Candace still left a lot of things inside of the trunk of the car. Eye felt that she really didn't have plans to stay as long as Eye expected or wanted her to stay or she was beginning to have reservations about marrying me. Candace came in and began setting her work computers up and connecting it to the internet so she could test it to see if things were working properly. When she ran into a snag Eye figured out the problem and everything started working properly. Candace and Eye started pinching ourselves to see if this was really taking place. Candace and my mother Janice got along really well. Prior to moving Candace up here we discussed living arrangements, as it was very important that Candace was comfortable. Eye didn't want her to relocate up here and couldn't adjust. Janice was going through a divorce settlement after being married forty-nine years and Eye was worried that Janice would have a nervous breakdown. Eye thought having Candace around would be a little easier because Eye know there were things Janice didn't want to talk to me about because Eye was her son, but she probably could better communicate with another woman that's been through a few divorces.

Candace and Eye would sleep next to each other every night. We'd make sure that we never went to sleep angry, upset or mad with each other. Candace lived for the attention and validation of social media. It was also a way for her to express whatever and however to get as much attention as possible. She loved to take pictures of her Brazilian butt lift, so the world could get a glimpse of her butt and breast job. Candace had her own office space where she wouldn't be disturbed and she could freely go to any part of the house and still be comfortable and feel at home. One week had gone by and we were still having a good time. A few minor adjustments had to take place because Candace wasn't used to cleaning up behind herself, throwing things in the trash or doing dishes that she used. Eye brought certain things to Candace's attention and she got an attitude but then she realized that Eye was only trying to help her adjust. Candace would put make up on or make a weave cap and leave traces of it without cleaning up behind herself. Eye can understand because she did the same thing at her home. Eye'm not saying she was dirty, but she didn't like to clean up much until she knew that Eye was coming to town.

One evening when Candace got off work we went to the casino and Eye won $3800.00. Eye gave Candace and Janice $100.00 each so they could continue playing. When Candace was out of money she came over to me and asked, "Can I borrow $500.00?" Eye replied, "No, Eye'm going to deposit this in my account." Candace got mad and walked away while calling me everything under the sun. When she came back around she sat next to me and Eye won another $600.00. Eye looked at Candace and said, "Eye've done all Eye can to help you out and you don't seem to ever have a problem getting mad and cussing me out when you don't get your way. Is that fair to me?" Candace said, "I'm sorry." Eye said, "here's the $500.00 you wanted to borrow. See, there's nothing Eye wouldn't do for you because Eye love you, but you must also understand that we still have obligations we have to meet for this wedding." Eye already paid for the banquet hall the wedding and reception was going to take place. Eye spent roughly $4000.00 for the wedding so far and all Eye received was a promissory note from Candace. Eye realized that Candace wasn't trying to pay her portion but was banking on the gifts we'd receive.

EYE'VE STOOD INSIDE THE EYE OF HELL AND REMAINED FEARLESS!

We'd find something to do every night so she'd at least get out of the house besides sitting in front of the computer for eleven hours {including overtime}. On this particular night Candace came downstairs already dressed, then she went upstairs to change two more times. Eye asked her, "why did you change so many times?" Candace said, "I didn't think you liked what I had on the first two times." Eye responded, "what you had on the first time was nice. Eye want you to be free to wear whatever you want." Eye reached up to hug Candace and she began to ball up in the corner saying, "what are you about to do to me? Please don't hurt me!" Eye immediately backed up five steps and asked her, "What's wrong? Eye've never done anything to hurt or harm you, have Eye? "No", Candace replied. Where did that come from? What's wrong with you?" Candace said, "it was a trigger." Eye constantly refreshed Candace's mind that Eye wasn't neither one of those guys from her past that hit, bit or punched her in her head. Eye started thinking that it was more to these stories than just triggers. Eye felt that Candace was on medication that she refused to take or bring with her because she knew Eye'd find out what it was for or treated. We still went out that evening and when we got back home Eye took my firearm off and placed it under my mattress, so it would be out of harms way. We cuddled and rested well with her head laying on my bare chest. When we awakened the next morning, Candace sat up and asked, "why did you say, you were going to put the gun to my head?" Eye flipped out and asked, "what the hell did you just say? Eye'd never put a gun to your head, where are you getting these things from? Have someone ever placed a gun to your head? Do you recall last December going hunting with me? Candace, Eye'll never hurt, harm nor hinder you." Candace looked at me with tears in her eyes and said, "I'm sorry, it was a trigger." Eye laid down and started thinking hard and meditating. Eye needed to talk with someone besides a family member because Eye didn't want anyone to look at Candace like she was crazy. Eye called my adopted brother and told him what happened. He asked me, "Is she bipolar or does she suffer from schizophrenia?" Eye replied, "Eye have no clue, but her sister during a conversation eluded to the fact that Candace had gone through something serious and traumatizing." My adopted brother, Danny asked me a serious question, "how well do you enjoy freedom? Whatever Candace is on or is going through is too much for you to handle or deal with. Your best bet will be to get her out of your house before you end up in prison being framed for rape or attempted murder. Eye got scared shitless, but he had a valid point. Eye always said, "my life and my freedom are my priorities and Eye refuse to allow anyone to jeopardize them.

Eye had so much on my mind that Eye had to analyze, but it didn't take away the fact that Eye really loved Candace. Eye had to weigh my options because these were life long decisions that Eye had to make. Eye knew that Candace was still very much tied to men from her past that she'd been sexually involved with but Eye wanted to be the person that would try and love all of her hurt and insecurities away. It was like Eye was living and singing that portion of Boyz 2 Men's song from "End of the Road":

"Girl I'm here for you
All those times of night when you just hurt me
And just ran out with that other fella
Baby I knew about it, I just didn't care
You just don't understand how much I love you do you?
I'm here for you
I'm not out to go out and cheat on you all night
Just like you did baby but that's all right
Hey, I love you anyway
And I'm still gonna be here for you 'till my dying day baby…"

The next morning, Candace's sister Leslie called twenty minutes prior to Candace starting work. Candace walked out of the room and talked with her while heading to the office. Eye got out of bed, showered got dressed and started doing laundry. Candace walked in the room where Eye was and brought her sarcasm with her. Eye guess her sister, Leslie was building her up to approach me in an offensive way. Leslie was Candace's makeshift protector and savior. The sad thing about Candace was she believed her sister loved her, but the truth of the matter was they pacified and covered up the truth to make

EYE'VE STOOD INSIDE THE EYE OF HELL AND REMAINED FEARLESS!

Candace believe something other than her reality. Leslie didn't want Candace happy so she did and said what she could to get her out of this relationship. Eye went down to the office to speak briefly with Candace about her sarcasm. Candace took her 15- minute break and all hell broke loose. Eye told Candace, "if you aren't happy here you could leave at any given moment. There's no strings attached and nothing's holding you here. You're interested in men that praise your body enhancement, yet you always ask me "Am I enough?" When in fact, Eye'm not and have never been enough for you. Give me my fucking ring and my key. Eye've had women with better natural bodies, than your purchased one. Eye can do better than you because Eye'm tired of you bringing me down and flipping out calling it a trigger."

Eye went back to finishing up the laundry and Candace started taking her work computers down. She was wearing stretch pants and a spaghetti strap tank top, no bra. She proceeded taking her things to her car and Eye asked her to respect me even if she refused to respect herself and put something over that see through top. She went upstairs and put a sweater on. Eye stood at the door and asked her, "are you leaving?" Candace stood in the corner of the room constantly repeating herself, "Lamont leave me alone." She had her phone in her hand and Eye said, "Eye don't care what you do or who you call, but you better not call the cops and lie on me, telling them that Eye'm harming you." Eye went downstairs and watched Candace get in her car, snatching her top off and driving away. Things didn't have to escalate to this level but Eye guess everything happens for a reason in its own season. Eye immediately called Candace to see if she'd answer but she ignored my calls. Eye called her mother to let her know what just transpired. Eye got in my car and drove around to see if Eye could locate Candace but didn't have any luck. Eye got back in the house and called her on video and Candace answered, looked in my face and hung up. Eye texted her, "well, you hung up on me so Eye'm guessing you don't want to talk to me, so have a safe trip.

Have you ever had a relationship with a paranoid schizophrenic?

Someone bipolar? Someone that has been molested and raped? What about someone that was married multiple times (ALWAYS playing the role of the victim)?

How about someone tremendously abused psychologically and emotionally that they create their own lies and believe them?

Well, Eye just had to completely and permanently cut it off with someone that endured all of the above.

Eye refuse to be lied on!!

My life and freedom are of equal importance and will NOT be jeopardized!!

We postponed the wedding because it was in our best interest to reevaluate things.

Eye NEVER would do any harm to a soul as a matter of fact she posted the great things Eye did for her. To see her spaz out hurt my heart because it let me know that she was still harboring junk in her head that was destroying her.

Months of being by her side helping her. Do you think Eye would have let her get on the road broke? Hell no.

Eye NEVER required all the money she owes me in one lump sum and Eye told her Eye'd gladly ship her things to her.

Eye'm so glad Eye dodged being married to a professional manipulator.

To all of my friends that have my best interest, Thanks for looking out for me!! – *Lamont Bershawn.*

EYE'VE STOOD INSIDE THE EYE OF HELL AND REMAINED FEARLESS!

Candace was making videos along the way to let social media know her every move and when she stopped to rest. Eye was concerned about Candace, but Eye wasn't going to ask her to comeback. Anyone that gets in their car and drive nineteen hours without money have a desire to be where they're headed or they're running to someone or running away from someone desperately. Candace called me on video chat the next morning at 7:17a.m. When Eye answered she said, "I love you Lamont." Eye responded, "Eye love you too baby. Where are you?" Candace replied, "I'm in a safe place. Can you send me my things?" Eye explained to Candace, "Eye didn't make you leave, you left because you wanted to. If you were going to head back home you had plenty of time to pack everything inside of your car. Send me money to send your things and its done. Meanwhile, don't forget that you owe me $1500.00." "All you're concerned with is the money I owe you, you're not worried about me!" "Again, you left on your own will and desire. Have a safe trip!"

Later that evening, Eye drove to the casino and Candace called me after as Eye arrived. Candace called me and said, "Hey Lamont! I made it home safely." Eye mean she acted like nothing ever happened. Eye said, "why in the hell did you put that lie on social media soliciting money from people as if Eye put you out of my home with no money and you had to immediately leave with just the clothes on your back?" Candace hung up on me. When Eye parked my car Candace's sister, Leslie called me with an attitude. Eye told Leslie, "you know your sister the drama queen, so calm down." Leslie calmed down and we had a civilized conversation. Leslie only heard Candace side of the story and got caught up in her emotions over what Candace said. Eye explained in detail what transpired between me and Candace. Leslie paused and said, "Oh okay, now I see where things went wrong. I told you Candace is fragile." Eye asked Leslie, "Is there something that Eye need to know. Eye've never experienced so many storms in one relationship. First, she began hyperventilating when she thought Eye was going to leave her. This time she balled up in the corner as if someone was about to beat her and Eye've never raised my hand to hit her or anything of the sort." Leslie got quiet for a moment and said, "Can I tell you something Lamont?" Eye said, "please do because Eye'm lost for words." Leslie said, "Candace was molested and raped at a very young age by a very close friend and family member. Our mother's way of dealing with the issue was to keep her in the church and let God deal with her. Lamont, I was hoping that you'd be the one to help heal her and take her mind into a place that there's still a few great men out here. You would have been her 4th husband and I was hoping that Candace wouldn't regress psychologically to that moment in her life that was destructive and suicidal. Candace's life took a turn for the worse a few years ago and she turned to Vodka, cocaine and became a sex addict for relief and love because she was hurting badly." "Thanks for sharing this with me Leslie. Now Eye know how to better deal with the situation. Is she on medication or has she learned to accept her reality and deal with it?" "Yes, Candace is on medication but she left it home because she didn't want you to know that she has a mental disorder."

Have you asked yourself, "Why am I in this relationship?" (2) "What am I doing wrong in my relationship?" (3) "Why did I ever get myself involved in this relationship?" (4) "What type of relationship is this?" (5) "Am I really ready for a relationship?"

Let's first define what a "Ship" is. A "Ship" is a vessel of considerable size for deep-water navigation.

Remember, there's a process in all things. The very first step before getting involved in a relationship or anything else is one MUST get off the "SLAVE SHIP!"

The "Slave Ship" is what holds people back from becoming KNOWN. On the Slave Ship people are (1) Living in FEAR (2) in a state/ condition of being confined (3) praying/ hoping for better to come FREE them because they're afraid to swim if they fall (4) Mentally Shackled, etc.

The 2nd Ship you'll arrive to is the "Acquaintanceship." The Acquaintanceship is the level of introduction. On this level, one must be interested in communicating.

The 3rd Ship is the "Courtship." On this level, both individuals enjoy the communication so much that they begin a "Courtship" which is the act of wooing each other intimately {NOT consisting of sex, but spiritual in nature}.

The 4th Ship one must arrive to is the "Fellowship." On this particular level, we've gotten a pretty great feel of each other now allow me to meet your friends/ family that you commune with daily. The "Fellowship" is when we acknowledge as of good standing, or in communion according to standards of faith and practice. In other words, we can respectfully blend.

The 5th Ship we'll arrive to is the "Partnership." On this particular level I'm placing my trust within you. The "Partnership" is when we're able to have joint possessions or interests.

The 6th Ship we'll arrive on is the beginning of a "Relationship." At this particular level we're able to relate spiritually, physically, emotionally, financially and psychologically. The "Relationship" begins when consideration has been taken on both sides to enter into an agreement to become deeper involved.

Have you gone through the process to REALLY become ONE? Are you ready to navigate deeper into the life of another? Is your "Ship" ready to sail or are you still tied to the dock? – Lamont Bershawn.

Leslie validated some of the things Eye had already previously thought and felt. It felt like a load of bricks had fallen on my chest at the same time Eye was relieved. While Eye was speaking with Leslie, Candace kept calling me but Eye wouldn't answer it for two reasons (1) Eye didn't feel like being hung up on and (2) Eye was getting to the bottom of what was actually wrong with Candace and Eye wasn't about to let that be interrupted.

Eye went home and so many things were on my mind so Eye had to lay down and meditate. Eye began packing up Candace's things and putting them in boxes so Eye could send a few at a time to her. Eye didn't return any of Candace's calls because Eye'd begun processing her out of my system completely. One evening, Candace called me and said, "I'm going to definitely pay you what I owe you. You didn't have to bail me out of my situations, so thank you." Another week had gone by and we still hadn't talked with each other. Eye'm not going to lie and say she wasn't heavily on my mind at times because she was. Early Saturday afternoon as Eye was sitting outside of the bank Candace called me and asked, "Can I see you?" Eye said, "of course." Candace called me on video and said, "I miss you so much Lamont and I'm ready to come home." Eye replied, "Eye miss you too. Are you sure you're ready to be solely with me?" Candace replied, "Lamont, since we've been together I've never been with anyone, even up to this point. Have you been with someone else?" "No Candace. What's surprising to me is the old me would have been with someone else. The love and respect Eye have for you prevented me from going that route."

Relationship 100:

> *"Once the trust is gone the relationship is over. Don't try to reconcile or try your best to work it out. You're wasting precious and valuable time beating a dead horse.*
>
> *When they tell you, "I'm going to change" that's bullshit to buy more time to Fuck you over!" – Lamont Bershawn.*

EYE'VE STOOD INSIDE THE EYE OF HELL AND REMAINED FEARLESS!

Two weeks later Janice was celebrating her 75th birthday and started planning a celebration like no other. Eye designed the invitations and Candace said, "since we're not getting married let's get the cake for this occasion." Candace asked, "Can I come to the birthday celebration?" Eye said, "Sure, if you'd like. Let me check prices for flights." Eye called Candace and said, "flights are $900.00, but Eye'm not paying that. The most Eye'll pay is half that." Candace immediately said, "I'll pay the other half. I'll give it to you when you pick me up from the airport." "Okay no problem." We began talking on a more frequent basis although Eye still hadn't forgotten what Leslie told me.

A few days later Eye picked Candace up from the airport. When Eye stepped out of the car to grab her luggage she hugged me tight and kissed me like she never wanted to let me go. When we arrived at the house Candace hugged my neck and cried saying, "I'll never leave you again. I should have gone into the other room and breathed instead of running away from a man that has done nothing but been exceptionally great to me. Will you forgive me?" "Eye've forgiven you when we began communicating again." We sat on the couch and Candace held my hand crying and asked, "Can I have my ring back?" Eye stood up and walked to my safe, opened it up and placed the ring back on her finger. Candace kissed me on the lips and then laid her head on my shoulder and said, "thank you for being my rock, the air that I breathe, my confidant and my soulmate." Eye responded with giving her a kiss on her forehead and a firm hug. Eye thought to myself, "what type of relationship am Eye in?"

There's all different "Types" of relationships. You have the:

(1) **PLATONIC RELATIONSHIPS,** *which are relationships that have no romance or sex.*
(2) **SURVIVAL RELATIONSHIPS,** *which are relationships that exist when partners feel like they can't make it on their own.*

(3) *VALIDATION RELATIONSHIPS, which are relationships when a person may seek another's validation of his or her physical attractiveness, intellect, social status, sexuality, wealth, or some other attribute.*

(4) *SCRIPTED RELATIONSHIPS which are relationships when they SEEM to be "the perfect pair," fitting almost all the EXTERNAL criteria of what an appropriate mate should be like. In other words, dealing with more "HELL" than they would like the public to know. This is one of the most dangerous/ deadly types of relationship.*

(5) *ACCEPTANCE RELATIONSHIPS which are relationships when two people ACCEPT trust, support and enjoy each other and their INDIVIDUALITY.*

(6) *INDIVIDUATION-ASSERTION RELATIONSHIPS are the relationships that are typically one-sided, but one person enjoys being admired while the other is throwing themselves at them.*

(7) *HEALING RELATIONSHIPS are relationships that follow periods of loss, struggle, deprivation, stress, or mourning. Participants typically feel wounded and fearful. They need TLC badly, and at the same time need to undertake some reassessment of themselves and their ways of relating.*

(8) *EXPERIMENTAL RELATIONSHIPS are those relationships where two people disagree more than agree but feel connected enough that they want to "try it out."*

(9) SEXUAL RELATIONSHIP is the relationship that is sexually based. In this type of relationship people become more possessive, more domineering & more physically/ mentally abusive. When engaging in sexual intercourse, there's a powerful bond that's being created {especially if it's the bomb diggity...lol}.

MOST relationships tend to reach this form because {A} the loss of interest in hopes of maintaining a connection through sex {B} Infidelity, the hope of gaining the power/ momentum to prevent it from ever happening again {C} Just the drawing power of the nature of it. Be mindful that a SEXUAL RELATIONSHIP is NOT always an INTIMATE RELATIONSHIP. An INTIMATE RELATIONSHIP is more of spiritual in essence but with ALL of the physical components. INTIMACY = Into - Me - See!!

There's many people that have met a person with a beautiful attitude, gorgeous body, but ugly as "Sin." What was supposed to be a one night of passion/ pleasure or stand turned into years of "SEXUAL BONDAGE." While being confined, isolated and incarcerated by "SEXUAL BONDAGE", you couldn't:

(1) be productive (2) travel freely (3) think clearly, etc.

WHAT TYPE OF RELATIONSHIP ARE YOU IN? *– Lamont Bershawn.*

We had a great time at Janice's birthday celebration. Eye let everyone know that Candace contributed to the party by purchasing the cake that was baked by the "Cake Boss." Candace took plenty of pictures and video footage so she could make Janice a memorable DVD.

A few days later Candace was leaving again. Eye said, "we're back at the stage that we hurdled and now how does it feel to you?" Candace replied, "I wish I'd never left in the first place." When Candace arrived back home she called me crying again stating, "it just doesn't feel right being here without you. I hate being here. When can I come home?" Eye told Candace, "you should have brought your work computers with you and you wouldn't have had to go back. We could have flown to get your car some other time, Eye mean we never go anywhere in your car anyway. Eye'll fly out to get you and we can drive back again in about a month, after Easter." Candace didn't like the sound of that and replied, "is it at all possible to come here before Easter? I want us to be at your house before Easter." Needless to say, Eye flew out there and Eye was shown another sign prior to getting in the car to hit the road. When Eye used the bathroom, Eye looked over in the shower and there was a bar of "Dove" on the ledge. Candace can't use anything other than "Ivory" soap. Eye asked Candace, "Is there something you want to tell me? Why is there a bar of "Dove" in the shower?" Candace said, "my daughter came over one night before she went out and brought her own soap over to shower with." Eye didn't believe her but there wasn't a reason to stay and argue. We got in the car and hit the road and drove non-stop to my home, arriving the Saturday before Easter.

We setup her work station in the office again and everything was working out really well between us. Eye actually overlooked a few things that once bothered me concerning Candace now that Eye understood a little of what took place in her life.

During her breaks Candace would come into the room where Eye was to check to make sure Eye was okay. Eye asked Candace, "if it would be too much to ask that we shut down our Facebook pages for a month to focus more on our relationship with each other?" Surprisingly, Candace agreed to shut her page down as Eye did as well. Ever so often, Candace would get back on Facebook which let me know that she still was very much tied to social media and needed the attention and validation from others, Eye felt that Eye no longer

EYE'VE STOOD INSIDE THE EYE OF HELL AND REMAINED FEARLESS!

mattered. Eye walked into the office and told Candace that the jeweler needed the ring for a couple of days in order to make the custom enhancer. Eye acted like Eye was taking it to the jeweler but instead Eye put it back in my safe and drove around the block to make her think that Eye went to drop the ring off.

Once again, Eye started feeling that it's useless to try to maintain any form of relationship with Candace. Eye also was wondering, "if she brought her medication with her this time." Candace received a phone call from her mother letting her know that everyone was coming into town because Candace's stepdad had stage four cancer and the doctors gave him less than one week to live. When Candace finished speaking with her mother, she came into the room with strands of tears in her eyes and she emphatically asked, "Lamont, hold me please! Hug me!" While Eye was hugging Candace, she burst into a loud scream and started crying." Eye began consoling her until she got herself together to get back to work.

The next morning, Janice and Eye had a meeting with her financial advisor. While we were in a meeting Candace called me and told me her stepfather just died. Eye gave her my condolences and said, "Eye'm on my way back home." When Eye got back to the house Eye asked Candace, "have you made flight arrangements to attend the funeral?" Candace asked, "Are you going to pay for my flight home for the funeral?" Eye said, "No, that's not my responsibility. Didn't you just get paid and won an additional $400.00 at the casino last night?" "All I have is $85.00", Candace said. "What happened to the money you won last night? Eye know you had it because Eye'm the one that cashed in the tickets for you." Candace got an attitude, so Eye walked away before things escalated. Candace came into the room where Eye was and Eye looked at her and asked her to give me the $85.00 and Eye proceeded to book her roundtrip flight. Candace said, "thank you. I also need money to buy something to wear for the funeral as well as my hair and nails done." Eye acted as if Eye didn't hear a word she was speaking. Eye kept telling Candace that Eye put money aside for our Vegas trip but she seemed to ignore that.

Eye asked Candace, "would you like me to go to the funeral with you for support?" Candace said, "No." Eye didn't argue with her as she had her reason for saying she didn't want me there. Candace said, "I'm staying at my mother's house and she's going to have a house full. We can't sleep together at my mom's house." Eye replied, "It's okay, my intention was to check in a hotel room anyway, but Eye'll stay here and wait for you to return."

Candace got off work and asked me, "when will my ring be done? I need to wear it and flaunt it at the funeral." "What do you mean you need to flaunt it at the funeral?", Eye asked. Eye know your first ex-husband will be there. Is it your intention to let him know and see that someone bought you a ring, in order to smear it in his face?" Candace said, "he probably can't see anything because he's considered to be legally blind." Eye didn't know him but just listening to her made me realize that this "b.i.t.c.h" is heartless, vindictive and full of drama.

What does "Hell hath no fury like a woman scorned" actually mean?

Considerably the belief in a literal place called "Hell" where those will go that denied, disrespected or blasphemed against their chosen God/ deity.

In Christianity, Hell is taught to be a place where these "bad" or unrighteous people will go covered by this lake of fire and can't ever die.

Anyone that understands the nature of a woman, she tends to absorb what she receives. This is why women are considered "receptors" and men are considered "projectors."

When an individual comes in contact/ connect to a bitter or scorned woman, one must understand it's something that penetrated her heart, mind, body and spirit to the point she placed herself in bondage over a circumstance that she refused to let go or heal from.

Men, understand that when dealing with a scorned woman you're going to pay

EYE'VE STOOD INSIDE THE EYE OF HELL AND REMAINED FEARLESS!

for/ be blamed for everything that happened prior to you coming into the picture. There's many physical signs such as, but not limited to: (1) enhancing their natural beauty {breast implants, ass shots, nose jobs, extensive plastic surgeries, etc.} Please understand that Eye'm NOT speaking about putting make up on.

There's some women that are pure B.I.T.C.H.E.S {Broke{n}/ Bitter Individuals Trying to Cause Havoc/ Hell Everyday Somewhere} and have had a screwed up or fucked up life{style} from birth. Their intentions are to make YOU feel obsolete, degrade you, paint a negative picture of you just because they're really no "Earthly Good."

Have you ever heard, "Misery LOVES Company?"

Just begin soaking, indulging or engaging in their atmospheres and you'll see just how contagious that shit really is. Some of you can vouch that you were doing extremely well until you allowed/ entertained that scorned individual.

BEWARE because she comes in ALL shapes and sizes, just awaiting the moment to turn into the BLACK WIDOW and devour your reputation!! – Lamont Bershawn.

My feelings were becoming bitter with Candace and Eye let it be known when she went to be with her family for the funeral. When Eye dropped Candace off at the airport, acted like she didn't want to kiss me. Eye had a lot of time to think about things while Candace was away. Eye felt Candace made plans to meet up with one of her previous sexual partners the reason she really didn't want me to fly with her or attend the funeral. Our conversations were tense at times and Eye told her, "you can stay there until Eye return from Vegas."

Candace said, "I'm looking forward to going to Vegas, I need a vacation." Little did she know, Eye was moments away from telling her to keep her conniving ass there as my feelings were diminishing towards her a great deal and Eye knew it was only a matter of time that this relationship would be over. Eye couldn't trust her anymore, yet Candace would always say, "if we'd ever break up it wouldn't be my fault or anything I would do." That was a major problem, Candace couldn't ever see what she was doing or causing. Was it because she wasn't taking her bipolar medication? Was it because she was trying to neglect her reality for a fantasy she was creating? Whatever it was, Eye knew that Eye had enough of dealing with it.

Don't ever deceive YOURSELF!!

YOU have aspirations, goals, ambitions, the power to dream, think & envision.

The moment you STOP is the moment you give your life away.

Your purpose is to make your dreams/visions a REALITY!!

BEWARE though because there are people that you've allowed in your circle that are listening to your ideas you're making public. These people are impostors whom you THOUGHT were your friends or close family members.

(1) Why are they stealing your ideas?
(2) Why have they decided to get closer to your "friends" and make them their very own?
(3) Why are they trying their best to dismember or degrade you behind your back?

ANSWER: Insecure "mutha fukkas" thrive on living in the confines of the lies they create for themselves and accept the lie as their real-

ity. **"NOTHING FROM NOTHING LEAVES NOTHING!"**

The people that makes the decision to be-LIE-ve them and connect with them are better off with them, TRUST ME!!

Iron sharpens iron as flies go hard for a pile of shit.

REMAIN FOCUSED or time will pass you by and you'll begin reflecting on your past only to realize that you've birthed so many millionaires or billionaires; but you're still at the beginning of the circle.

You've been wondering why you've been seeing the same old things, attracting the same type of folk and engaging in the same old conversations without evolving in your travels.

You've been on a solar powered Ferris wheel and didn't know it.

This is YOUR time, YOUR NOW.... MAKE YOUR LIFE WORK for YOU!

When situations occur that relieve you of some folk, ACCEPT IT!! Don't ask questions, don't get upset, don't argue, don't cry, don't worry but be EXTREMELY HAPPY.

The vindictive will easily connect with its kind as with the schizophrenic, the liar and deceiver. The reason it's NOT so easy to connect with you is because your innermost radar can pick up on their bullshit! – Lamont Bershawn.

When Candace arrived back here after being away for the funeral, she hugged and kissed me and got in the car. As soon as we got home, Eye brought her bags upstairs and she immediately began sucking my dick. Candace paused and said, "please don't ever take my love for granted or downplay my true feelings for you." She bent over while taking her pants and panties off. This was the first time Eye smelled her ass stinking. She laid a towel on the bed, laid on top of it and pulled me on top of her. She was having an orgasm and she wanted me to cum inside of her and Eye did. Candace asked me, "why did you squint or frown when you entered inside of me?" Eye had to tell her, "it's because your ass is stinking." Candace laughed it off and proceeded to the bathroom to get a shower. Later that evening, we began packing for Las Vegas. Eye allowed Candace to go since the trip was already paid for five months in advance. This was the last hurrah, either things were going to change drastically in Vegas or things would be over between us when we returned.

We arrived in Vegas and went shopping because we were going to be there for one week. We slept in the same bed, but didn't have sex or make love, we didn't cuddle, we didn't take a shower together, we didn't dialogue like we used to, we didn't laugh while spending alone time in the same room. Evidently, we didn't feel the same towards each other anymore. When we got back on the airplane heading back home Eye knew it was just a matter of time before we'd permanently end whatever strings was left keeping the relationship together.

When we got back to the house, Eye brought all of the bags out of the car and Candace didn't want to help. While Eye was bringing in the bags, she went to the room and laid on top of the covers in her dirty clothes. Eye came upstairs and asked her, "to either get washed or a shower and put her pajamas on if she wasn't feeling well." Candace sarcastically said, "I'm not doing anything." When Eye walked to the other side of the bed Candace jumped up and went downstairs. Eye thought she was in the office or the den watching television. Eye got showered up and got in the bed and took a long nap. When Eye awakened Eye was a little hungry so Eye ordered two large pizzas. Eye went downstairs to check on Candace and she was watching television. Eye told her the food would be there shortly. Candace ate when the food arrived but said very little to me. Eye went back upstairs and laid back down as Eye felt drained.

Approximately 11 p.m. Eye went downstairs to see if Candace was okay. Eye looked everywhere and didn't see her and her car was still outside. Eye went to the bathroom door downstairs and the door was closed and locked. Eye knocked on the door and no answer. Eye called her phone and still didn't get an answer. Eye thought to myself, "Eye hope this girl didn't commit suicide in my house. Eye started to take the door off the hinges and Candace unlocks the door as if she just woke up. Eye looked at her and said, "If you no longer want to be with me or if you're afraid of me then you need to pack your car and get out of my house." The next day after she got off work Candace packed her vehicle. Eye asked her, "was she leaving?" Candace didn't respond. Eye said, "If you're leaving make sure you pack everything and don't come back. Just remember you owe me $600.00, so Eye'll create the agreement so we can sign it and my mother can witness it. Candace called her mother and acted like someone was doing something to her. Eye said, "Eye can see why you've been married so many times. It's because you're too damaged to be by yourself so your intention or motive is to fuck up other people's lives because you're not happy with your own life. Eye knew it was a mistake allowing you to come back." Candace signed the agreement, left and said, "Goodbye!"

Two days later, Candace called me {Eye didn't know that she was still in town} but she asked, "Lamont, can I borrow $200.00 to get my car home. Please don't tell anyone that I called you." Eye responded, "why don't you ask the person that put you up in the hotel for the money. Eye'm going to stick to our agreement and not get deeper in debt with you because Eye want this connection or attachment to be lost and over. One week after our conversation Eye received a text from Candace with the code from Walmart to Walmart to pick up the money she owed me. Two minutes after Eye text her that Eye received the money she called me to thank me for everything. Eye told her that Eye'm hoping the best for her and sorry we didn't work out. One week after that Candace called me while she was getting a manicure and pedicure asking me about a cd that Eye made for her when we initially met. Eye told her to enjoy it and remember me. "Lamont I'll never forget you!", Candace replied.

Please understand that your spirit is ALWAYS in protective mode. This is why it's important and IMPERATIVE to be in tune with your consciousness.

The moment you question yourself or your action to allow your flesh or belief to give an answer, you'll realize that evil is always present in your space or circle.

It's waiting the opportune time to devour you. This is why you must beware of the decoy that will distract you in order to set you up for destruction.

S/N: A "distraction" will be a disruptive disturbance that takes your focus away

from anything important. This is why some of you have become sidetracked and it has caused years of delay with your promise. (Eye feel like preaching)

The essence of who you are will NEVER disconnect from the source. You're powerful beyond what anyone can see. Remember, the "enemy" gains your power by connecting to the "inner me" and drains your "energy" by intoxicating your "inner-G!" – Lamont Bershawn.

On June 2, 2018, Eye received another call from Candace. She began asking me questions as if Eye immediately jumped into another relationship. A few of the questions let me know that she and Jerome had been talking because it's the same lie he's been telling women that Eye was no longer involved with for years. Eye set the record straight with Candace and asked her to never contact me again.

Many years ago, people would tell me that Jerome was jealous of me, envious of me and wanted to be just like me but Eye refused to accept what people told me because we're actually siblings. Eye remember being at Kurt's first wedding and Jerome's girlfriend was speaking with my fiancée and she told her that Eye was the better acting and looking twin.

EYE'VE STOOD INSIDE THE EYE OF HELL AND REMAINED FEARLESS!

Eye often wondered why Jerome was so competitive when it came to me and why he felt the need to "throw shade" or do his best to tell lies to these women to get them to all of a sudden jump on his bandwagon. Eye realized that most of these women were hurt that Eye made the conscious decision to walk away from them but Eye never abandoned or disrespected them. It was either Eye felt that we no longer had anything in common, they were more of a "knife" instead of "wife material" or Eye realized they were extremely damaged by previous relationships and had countless "triggers" that still haunted them.

What Eye've realized is that Eye truly dodged a bullet when Eye walked away from Candace because she had a motive to seduce my intellect in order to devour me and have me sent to prison. What Candace didn't know was that Eye constantly did a spiritual and physical cleanse because Eye knew she was full of filth. The reason she was married three times was due to the fact her parents never took the time to give her the necessary attention or validated her, so every man she met she found herself sexually involved with. Candace never had a man like me enter her life to express so much respect, allowed her voice to be heard and literally honored her.

Since my involvement with Candace, Eye've learned to question myself. As a matter of fact, anyone making a choice to begin a relationship should ask yourself:

> *How well do you know the person you're with {spouse, mate, companion, significant other, lover, etc.}?*
> *Would they ever betray you?*
> *Would/ Could they be there or by your side if you really needed them?*
> *Would/ Could they vouch for your character in a positive way?*
> *Would they be willing to give up a kidney or blood if you were a match and needed them?*

Could it be you thought you "KNEW" them, only to realize that you've been "Sleeping with the enemy" the entire time?

POINT: Circumstances/ situations alter people's perceptions, interpretations and lives daily. The person you're giving the "Mantle of Trust" to, could be the very one that's jealous/ envious of you! – Lamont Bershawn

Ladies and Gentlemen:

Please pay strict attention and be aware of your surroundings. In this moment of your life you're being challenged to make sound decisions.

The decision you're about to make will either catapult you into a successful place or give you years of delay with your blessing because you're not ready to receive what has already been promised.

Be careful because the enemy is going to send a DECOY to DISTRACT your "INNER-ME" in order to set you up for DESTRUCTION!

Remain in tuned with the "INNER-G" in your circle. Anything draining your energy is a compromising or conflicting force that must be removed because it will end up killing you.

How did the conflicting force get into your circle? It arrived at a vulnerable point in your life with its very own motive to seduce you. Your heart received them while your spirit was protecting your every move, giving you the strength to finally see what was in the midst of your company.

POINT: You're standing too close to the mirror. Back away from the mirror so you can get a clear view of what and who's surrounding you

"Often times people get upset during a relationship or after the break up. It's natural and okay to become emotional and even feel a little resentment.

EYE'VE STOOD INSIDE THE EYE OF HELL AND REMAINED FEARLESS!

> *As some church folk would say, "don't tarry too long."*
>
> *Face it, some folk are so used to dealing with trash therefore don't know how to value a treasure when they've received one." – Lamont Bershawn.*

Eye'm truly thankful for my spiritual evolution that have allowed me to see each and every entity and recognize their intention or motive. Eye'm also thankful for those "roots" in my life that have my best interest at heart. Eye want everyone to know that Eye haven't come to the realization that Eye'm perfect but Eye've come to a point in my life that Eye'm able to speak to my presence as well as my atmosphere.

Just in case you haven't recognized who Eye'm,

EYE AM:

> *Lamont, the Author of a best seller, "Bishops Need Love Too."*
>
> *Lamont, the dedicated friend that will be there for you until the very end.*
>
> *Lamont the Man: would love to get to know her heart, her mind, what makes her feel certain ways. Why she holds her head certain ways, why she tends to cringe at certain times, why does she cry in the midst of sleeping, etc.*
>
> *Lamont the former Pastor: is the person that's concerned with your well-being. Whether or not you'd even allow me to take you to the next level spiritually.*
>
> *Lamont the lover: is concerned with all the above as well as preparing to meet the sexual, emotional, financial & psychological needs of the woman in my life. Making sure Eye make love not only to her body, but also to*

her mind. Letting her know that every moment we're together {in physical/ spiritual} moments that she'll never have anything to worry about. Eye'm her protector, her lover, her friend, and her confidant. No battle is too much, no war is to in depth, and the sky is the limit.

Lamont the "Satanist" {NOT devil worshiper}: the bringer of knowledge.

Lamont the "Non- believer": to be-LIE-Ve means that one really don't know.

Lamont the "convicted murderer": Yes, Eye'm sure this one got a lot of attention. When Eye was the Pastor, "I" took upon the job/ duty of the slave master to "kill" the minds of the people while leading them deeper into slavery/ bondage. Outside of the church, "I" also got into disagreements/ arguments with people and went for the "jugular vein." Some of you are still doing so. It was upon my conviction by "Wisdom" that Eye've decided to leave the church in order to set the captives free. It was also "Wisdom" that taught me to express more love and humility even in the midst of a disagreement. A person can only live according to that which was taught to them.

Lamont the "Prophet": Eye can bet many of you had no idea that you carry this "title" too. Allow me to show you. Have you ever said any of these things to yourself? (1) This is the last time I'll be going through this? (2) This is the last year I'll be broke, busted and disgusted? (3) I'm going to get up off my ass and make this thing work for me? I'll never get myself involved in another relationship like this? Well, you've just spoken things into YOUR OWN life "Prophet{ess}!!"

EYE'VE STOOD INSIDE THE EYE OF HELL AND REMAINED FEARLESS!

S/N: Most of you {that are on my friends list} are very intelligent and Eye too have probably learned something from you. You may NOT have the "alphabet/acronym" attached to your name but share your thought provoking topics fit for a book/ blog. Stop wasting all of it on Facebook.

After all the above mentioned, that's still just a fraction of the "hats" you wear that will NEVER completely define who you are.

EYE AM Lamont Bershawn and Eye'll ALWAYS be "M.E!" {Metaphysically Evolving}!!

Aye, Aye

THE GREATEST PART OF LIFE besides being able to help or teach someone how to better themselves is learning exactly who you are, the purpose of your struggles and the power you possess from within. Eye can honestly say that through my trials, tribulations, setbacks and hurdles Eye've finally been able to say, "Aye get it!"

> *"Aye" was common in dialect and is the formal word for voting "yes" in the <u>United Kingdom House of Commons</u>.*
>
> *The most common use of "Aye aye, sir" is as a naval response indicating that an order has been received, is understood, and will be carried out immediately[2]. It differs from "yes", which, in standard usage, could mean simple agreement without any intention to act. In naval custom, a reply of "yes sir" would indicate agreement to a statement that was not understood as an order or a requirement to do anything. The alternatives of "aye aye sir" and "yes sir" would allow any misunderstanding to be corrected at once. This might be a matter of life and death for a ship at sea.*
>
> *Basically, it means that the speaker understands and will obey a direct order.*

EYE'VE STOOD INSIDE THE EYE OF HELL AND REMAINED FEARLESS!

Aye = Yes, that is correct.
Aye Aye = I understand, and will comply.
{Wikipedia definition}

In this particular passage, "Aye" means "YES, Eye get it or YES, Eye understand it."

For every lie that was told on me, "Aye" get it. The person was intimidated by my presence or my walk that they felt the need to lie on me in order to give their ego a boost.

Did it work? Absolutely Not! You still had to deal with the reality of your situation and telling lies on me didn't make it any better.

The entire time Eye was a part of a religious organization and later felt the need to depart, "Aye" get it. Eye had to go through the process of learning what religion and church was all about so Eye could properly inform people of the scam and the truth.

Did it work? As Eye put out information concerning religious be-"LIE"-f systems, people are beginning to receive "revelation" and answers within their own spirit. Eye remain humbled along this journey called life as Eye continue to be a student as well as a teacher. Eye respect everyone's walk, spiritual journey and religious views as it has never been my intention to change, coerce, convince, conquer or manipulate the minds of people.

Eye've come to the conclusion that sometimes parents don't have their child's best interest at heart. Why did my father hate me so much? "Aye" get it. It's because Eye was the only child that wasn't a whore or womanizer like him. My eldest brother followed in his footsteps and landed a double-life prison sentence.

BRAIN TEASER:

{Something that should make YOU THINK}!!!
If the "Biblical God" (1) own EVERYTHING in the world (2) is powerful beyond measure (3) have the power to SPEAK to anything and it MUST obey but (4) also

have a human emotion that it too can become jealous.

Eye ASK:

Why was it NECESSARY for "God" to sacrifice "his only begotten son {child}?"
The answer is in the above statement.
Just like some of YOUR parents/Guardians are jealous or envious of YOU.
It's the ONLY LOGICAL answer as to why an omniscient, omnipresent and omnipotent "God" would do such a thing.
TRUTH:
Some of your very own parents will make it hard for you to succeed in life, even when they have the keys to an open door for you. It's sad, but VERY TRUE!!
Just because they're considered your parents don't always mean they desire the best for you out of life. It doesn't mean you have to disrespect or dishonor them in any way.
Changing your name will not dismember or disconnect you because the fact still remains those are your parents.

PARENTS {THAT LOVE YOUR CHILD{REN}:

WOULD YOU SACRIFICE YOUR CHILD'S LIFE FOR ANYTHING?

POINT: NO loving parent will sacrifice their child. The next time someone tells you, "For God so loved the world..." and sees the bible as God's love letter. You have MY permission to tell them, "YOU'RE PSYCHOLOGICALLY

EYE'VE STOOD INSIDE THE EYE OF HELL
AND REMAINED FEARLESS!

FUCKED AND NEED HELP!!" – *Lamont Bershawn*

The church is said to be a "hospital" where healing takes place. Eye found it to be a place where so many secrets are capable of being hidden, a safe haven for the pedophile and a place where people can continue lying to themselves. Just look and notice how many Catholic Priests and male Pastors of different faith have regularly molested the altar boys or young men because of their powerful position and influence.

Why is it dangerous to join ANY religious organization?

Religious organizations are one of many groups that will accept you in, cater to you, consider you family and wait the opportune time to destroy you.
Religion {Re-LIE-Jun} is a bullshit belief system that was created to (1) make one deny their own spirituality (2) confuse people to the point that they rely on something outside of themselves (3) degrade the intellect of SELF (4) prepare oneself for an Insane Asylum by becoming institutionalized (5) teach people how to become imprisoned in their own minds!
While doing so, you've just accepted an oath and obligation to defend a created god with your natural life. How fucked up is that?
Most pew dwellers will never understand this because it's easier to keep someone else "seemingly" responsible for the choices or decisions that you make through a be-LIE-f system.
Have you ever met/ seen a musician later become a Pastor? Eye guess many of you want to know the REAL reason behind it. It's the

musician's duty to keep up with the Pastor's sermon and know just when to emotionally get the congregation involved. These people actually do most of the hard work, but never gets compensated like the orator.

At any cost, you no longer can be yourself, but now must go along with the "play book" or DESIGNED curriculum to swindle your congregants by any means necessary. It's fairly easy, all you have to do is profess, believe and sell the non-existent product.

Be EXTREMELY careful!! People are ready and willing to assassinate you and your character by going against it or denying it!

In conclusion:

Eye've been crucified by some of the closest people to me, those that Eye once considered family. Eye was burned at the stake by those Eye once called friend.

LISTEN UP!!!:

Don't invite me to your church, if you don't want the TRUTH!! Eye had enough of going to churches and the Pastors telling me what THEY WANTED ME to preach about - FUCK YOU!!

Don't invite me on your talk show, if you expect to bridle my tongue!!

Don't include me in your FB posts, if you don't want me to get "deep" or write my view on the topic!!

Don't invite me to any affair, if you expect me to be fake!!

Don't ask me any questions, if YOU don't want my truth with a well written explanation/ statement!!

EYE'VE STOOD INSIDE THE EYE OF HELL AND REMAINED FEARLESS!

Don't bring me in court on a fucking lie, Eye'll make EVERYONE look at you like the fool you are!!

Don't attempt to slander my name because of your insecurities, Eye'll make you more infamous than you could ever imagine with the TRUTH!!

Whoever you are, wherever you might fit in Eye just want to take this time to let ALL of YOU know......

My name is Lamont Bershawn and "Eye Refuse to Bust Hell Wide Open!!"

Acknowledgements

To my loving mother, Dorothy Burno. You're the first Goddess that Eye recognized. You carried me a full life term without ever giving up on me. It was through your pain that Eye saw the real strength to never give up on my dreams or visions. You taught me that life was valuable and Eye only had one to live, so make my stamp on the world. Thank you for loving me and giving me the best gift anyone could receive, LIFE!! Eye'll always love you mom!!

To my "Brother from another mother", Alexander Hardy. Words could never explain my heartfelt gratitude and appreciation. You tend to bring the joy and laughter out of me even in the midst of my heartache and pain. The countless number of hours that were spent on the phone was always uplifting. You painted a clear picture of my path when it all seemed so blurry. We have so much in common that you even began accepting my mother as your very own. Eye appreciate you from the bottom of my heart brother.

To my "Big Brother", Dr. Dennis Spencer. You've been a blessing for nearly the thirty years Eye've known you. You've hurdled obstacles that should've grounded you, yet when the dust cleared you were still standing. Eye appreciate you, Doc!

To my nieces, Alexis and Keonni. You two have grown into mature ladies and Eye'm very proud of you both. You have the power within you to create a wonderful destiny.

EYE'VE STOOD INSIDE THE EYE OF HELL AND REMAINED FEARLESS!

To my nephews, Demetri and Brandyn. You young men have made me proud. When neither of your fathers would acknowledge you or sought to help you, Eye was there. Eye'm grateful that you both accepted me with opened arms.

To my extended family, The Barg-Walkow family. Words will never be able to express my appreciation for all of you. Thanks so much for exemplifying the meaning of love and loyalty.

To my Deceased family, Mama Linda, Gramps and Uncle Tim. Eye'll never forget you and the things you've taught me. You'll always be in my heart and on my mind. Eye love you!!

To all of my friends on social media and surrounding areas. Thanks so much for your patience, love and support!!

A very special thanks to my artists Neusi Kesho and Maurice Powell.

Dedication to Lamont

*I*DON'T KNOW WHAT I'VE DONE *in my life to be so blessed. I had a brother named Daniel, when I was forty years old he passed. I met a man named Thomas and a man named Lamont. I didn't know when I met them they'd become my new brothers. I never had a younger brother and I never knew what it would feel like to have a healthy older and younger brother. For my brother Daniel had been sick his entire life.*

I'm not a wise man, but I'm smart enough to see the working of the Almighty when its produced before my eyes. To my eyes, so clearly as through the actions of my two brothers to me. Their kindness and self-effacing couldn't have been through any agency but the Lord.

The love, kindness and compassion shown to me by these two men not of my own blood is all the proof I'll ever need of the province of the Almighty! Amen.

Always remember, "money don't solve a thing, people do!"

I've met you at my tenth hour, Bishop Bershawn. I wished I would've met you at the beginning of my first. I have met Jewish Rabbis whom I loved immensely. I've met ministers and priests mostly of Catholic or Baptist faith. I've lived in an age where foolish whites hated those with black skin.

As an old dying white man, I've never met anyone who have given me so much love of the Almighty than you, Bishop Bershawn.

EYE'VE STOOD INSIDE THE EYE OF HELL AND REMAINED FEARLESS!

{I'm truly a foolish man because I was afraid of your embrace}!!

What a fine, loving and devoted brother you are. You are my brother as well as my Bishop!! – The Late Alexander Hardy.

www.ingramcontent.com/pod-product-compliance
Lightning Source LLC
Chambersburg PA
CBHW070054080526
44586CB00013B/1058